COPARENTING WITH CHRIST

COPARENTING WITH CHRIST

9 Steps to Achieving Harmony

DR. CHANEL A. SERANO

XULON PRESS

Xulon Press
2301 Lucien Way #415
Maitland, FL 32751
407.339.4217
www.xulonpress.com

Unless otherwise indicated, Scripture quotations taken from the Holy
Bible, New International Version (NIV). Copyright © 1973, 1978, 1984,
2011 by Biblica, Inc.™. Used by permission. All rights reserved.

Paperback ISBN-13: 978-1-6628-0832-6

Ebook ISBN-13: 978-1-6628-0833-3

Table of Contents

Jesus looked at them and said, "With man this is impossible, but not with God; all things are possible with God" (Mark 10:27).

Introduction

GOD PLACED A LOVE AND A PASSION IN MY heart for God's daughters. Women are an integral part of our society, our families, and our homes. We play a significant role in the type of legacy we choose to leave behind for our children and generations to come. With this in mind, this treasure focuses on parenting, but it pushes you to delve further into the woman underneath being a mother. What do I mean? You will know soon enough!

This is the kind of book you read when the kids are at school and you find yourself at a local eatery with your bottled water, tea, or coffee, watching others skip to the beat of fast-paced America. You are dressed casual and comfy at a table by yourself with your sword (Bible) and a journal next to you, with a pen in hand, ready for little nuggets of wisdom to hit you, and for those moments when God whispers in your spirit.

I prayed for you. As my fingers swiftly, yet methodically typed these words, I thought about you, the one reading this book, the one who has spent nights crying in her pillow, wondering how she was going to pay that gas bill tomorrow as her little ones slept in the next room. I prayed about you as you find yourself entering a new chapter in life, may it be academically, professionally, or spiritually. You are not alone in this feat; despite the many attempts of the enemy to distract you, to keep you in fear, worry, and anxiety, God has designed you to persevere and to finish this race triumphantly!

Ladies, I know it can be challenging at times with trying to balance family, work, home, school, and the many other areas in our lives. Please know that God sees you pushing forward, fighting through, and this season (that's right, just a season) will soon pass. God is your provider. He is your healer, your restorer, your comforter, and your biggest fan.

Life is a faith journey. God never said that it was going to be easy, but through His promises, we will get through the bumps and challenges. God has a purpose for you, specifically designed for you. Do not allow circumstances to keep you from your God-given purpose. It is time to re-adjust your crown, ladies, and let's get to work!!!

Part One

Developing the Character of God

Being the leader of a single mothers' ministry blesses me with an opportunity to hear of other mothers' experiences as a solo parent. I began to understand the many similarities, differences, trials, and joys of women who had one concept in common: faith. This opened my heart to the desire of exploring another side of the Christian single-mother experience, which was their emotional well-being. As I conducted a review of literature to prepare for my doctoral study several years ago, text upon text and study after study shared findings involving the negative impact of single parenting on children such as poor behavior, poor school attendance, poor academic records, high rates of or higher risk of incarceration, crime, substance use and abuse, and gang involvement. In some cases, the findings indicated the negative impact of single parenting on the mother. Yet, very limited research had been conducted on the intersection of single-mothering, faith, and emotional well-being. My doctoral study provided several important findings and led to my wanting to take the study to another level with writing this book.

Emotional well-being is the quality of one's daily experience. The emotional well-being is a vital part of creating a healthy lifestyle and a positive mindset to be successful in life, especially for single mothers. One's faith journey has an overall positive impact on a single mother. This refers to your relationship with Christ. One's ability to develop healthy emotional well-being involves one's ability to create harmony in their life. Harmony can be described as peace, consonance, in one accord, fluidity of various roles in one's life. In achieving harmony, one must be open to understanding that it is a journey that is comprised of several steps. Each of these steps are covered in the chapters of this book. Part 1 provides the foundation for creating harmony in your life with the initial step being identity. Chapter one explores the essence of identity beyond how the world defines identity, but how it is defined by God. Furthermore, this chapter helps you to gain clarity and wisdom on identity and the difference between identity and the many roles that we play as women. Steps to harmony begin with creating a solid foundation, and a solid foundation starts with knowing who you are in Christ. A solid identity in Christ helps one to stay grounded and rooted to the source, and this relationship with God contributes to having trust, faith, and peace in your life. This is an essential part of harmony.

We then move deeper into Part 1 as we step into chapter two, where we delve into how understanding your God-designed purpose, vision, and mission is an important step in not only understanding who you are in Christ, but how these three concepts contribute to achieving harmony in your life. The foundation to creating harmony in life is reached when you have spiritual clarity on why you are here, what your purpose is on earth, and how God has called you to glorify Him and serve His children.

Chapter 1

Who Are You?

"God created mankind in His own image, in the image of God He created them; male and female He created them" (Genesis 1:27 NIV).

GO AHEAD! TAKE A MOMENT AND ANSWER that question. Who are YOU? A mother, a daughter, an employee, a student, a volunteer, a social worker, a teacher, an entrepreneur. This list can go on and on. Did you notice how your response was based on relation to others? Let us try this one on for size. How about... a prayer warrior, a daughter of the King, a daughter of the Most High God, a Proverbs 31 woman, a life-changer, a motivator, an encourager, an intercessor, an agent of change? It is a paradigm shift, indeed, but one that is needed by all women.

Women have been created to be in relation and connection with others. Women are oftentimes known as the one who keeps the house physically and emotionally intact, ensuring that the home is immaculate, the children are well tended to, dinner is on the table by 5 sharp, 572 cupcakes are baked with handwritten holiday messages for the school bake sale for the following morning, all while you prepare a week's worth of dinner for a friend whose husband is recovering from foot surgery. Granted, this may appear to be an exaggeration, however, it depicts the image of what society has created as the ideal woman. One who is tending to the needs of others, even if it results in poor self-care, or worse, little or no private time with God. Before we can move forward, let's first have a conversation about identity versus roles. Now, of course, when I ask you this question, we have a tendency to think the two concepts are one in the same. But are they really?

Identity versus Roles

Are you intrigued? Identity versus roles is an interesting concept. Is there a difference between identity and role? Are the two somehow intertwined? This is a fundamental concept that one must grasp before moving forward in any capacity, whether it is as a mother, employee, or PTA member. Imagine the following: a vertical line with you on the lower end and God on the top; the horizontal line represents your relationship with others with you on one end, and the others on the opposite end. So often, we confuse the two lines of relationships. Identity is who you are in Christ and provides the foundation of one's existence. Whereas the term, *role* refers to a position you play in relation to others. We, as women, play many roles: the role of mother, the role of daughter, ministry leader, or a teacher, for example. However, contrary to popular belief, these roles do not define who we are. When we understand this distinction, we are then able to not only prioritize the importance of each role, but we will be able to perform these roles more efficiently.

This is the first step in achieving harmony in life as a single mother is to learn, develop, and understand who you are in Christ. Understanding how having a solid identity as a daughter of God opens the door to achieving harmony among the various roles that you play and areas that you tend to in your life.

Thinking back in my own life, I had to question when it first hit me that who I was as a daughter of the King was different from who I was as a mother, social worker, and ministry leader. I was preparing for a meeting for our single moms' ministry, and

God began downloading, as I like to call it when God begins pouring His vision into my heart. God gave me a vision on how to serve mothers by delving into and teaching on the "how tos" of preparing for their purpose. As this series began to unfold in my spirit, my first thought was, what is the first step in preparing for your purpose? It is your answer to the question, who are you? You see, at the time, I was a doctoral student, a social worker with a high caseload, a mother, single moms group facilitator, and the list went on and on. At that moment, these positions, although positions I valued, were roles that I played, but who was I at the core before these roles came to be? Who did God see before I was even a thought in my parents' hearts? God reminded me of this Scripture:

"Are not five sparrows sold for two pennies? Yet not one of them is forgotten by God. And even the very hairs of your head are all numbered, do not be afraid: you are worth more than many sparrows" (Luke 12:6-7).

Some years ago, I had a conversation with an older gentleman. He was very active, independent, mobile at one time, and due to a recent accident, was now in a wheelchair. He was living with depression, and as I was sitting there chatting with him, tears began flowing down his cheeks. He said, "I have no worth, I have nothing, I am nothing." His daughter, not sure what to say, began crying. I reached out my hand and placed it over his, declaring the Word over his life, reciting this Scripture. I looked at him and said, "God has a purpose for you. Yes, you worked in construction. Yes, you were a driver and a volunteer, but these are roles, they don't define who you are or who you belong to. You've been bought with a price, and who you are is a son of the Most High God, you are an ambassador of Christ, you have been created with purpose and created on purpose. God has so much more for you to do, so stop limiting yourself based on your circumstances." He wiped his tears, smiled, and from that moment, moved forward, with God leading him.

You see, if only we knew who we were in Christ, just think of how different life would be. If you knew who you were in Christ, down to the core and the very essence of God on the inside of you, how would your decision-making process change? Would you have made some of the choices that you made if you had? This is not a shaming moment, this is an awakening, one in which when we know better, we do better. You are created on purpose and with purpose. Whether you were born from a one-night stand, single-parent household, a planned pregnancy, or conceived by a married couple....God knew you and was amazed at who He has called you to become. Stop doubting yourself. It's time to walk in Him and for Him.

Now, let us shift gears and explore your relationship with Christ. Perhaps we should take a step back and explore whether you have a relationship with Christ, then we will explore what that relationship looks like. Here are a few questions to ponder as we delve into your relationship with God: What are your core beliefs and values? What is your philosophy on life? Do you believe in the age-old controversy of nature versus nurture? What is your worldview or the lens in which you see the world? Perhaps you have a scientific worldview, one that is based on scientific theory or evidenced-based and solely dependent on facts. Perhaps you have a biblical worldview that is based on the Bible. What do you believe about God and who He is? What do you believe is our purpose here on earth, both collectively and individually? Well, we shall get into that more in chapter two; however, it is a question to ponder when thinking of identity. Knowing your thoughts, feelings, and responses to the aforementioned questions may begin to open your heart to who you are.

Identity in Christ provides the very foundation from which we live. It is the core of every element of our lives. Identity involves how God sees you when He created you. It is not how you see yourself, but how God sees you and what He says about you, His beloved. Praise God, that God sees us through His eyes and not through our eyes. Oftentimes, as women, we can have such a distorted view of true beauty, God's beauty. Societal pressures, cultural and family views, and global ideals may dictate how we view ourselves internally, externally, and eternally. It is time that we take back the reigns and allow God to determine who we are. How do you view yourself? Ask yourself whether your response is genuine, is it a view engrained in us by others, such as parents, society, and culture? At times, family, friends, and loved ones mean well, but we must remember that if it does not align with the Word of God, then it is important to reject it. Do not misunderstand, I am not anti-family, but we must guard our hearts and be mindful on what we receive in our spirit. When you describe yourself internally (thoughts, feelings) and externally (physically), what words do you *choose* to use? We must commit to having a paradigm shift in how we see and love ourselves.

How to Strengthen Your Identity

My hope is that you have a clear understanding of the distinction between role and identity. Allow us to peel back a layer or two to get to the root of identity in Christ: your relationship with God. How one strengthens their identity begins with establishing, developing, and strengthening your relationship with Christ. It is assumed that if you are reading this book, that you have a level of spiritual knowledge and a connection with God. But fact and assumptions are two different concepts, so let us be sure! Oftentimes, we confuse religion (a man-made institution often guised as rituals, list of dos and don'ts, and radicalism) and a relationship with Christ (a genuine connection emerging from being a born-again believer). I know the latter statement was powerful, left a lasting impact, and probably left you with some questions and possibly evoked some interesting emotions. In addition to not only reading, but studying your Bible, fasting, journaling, prayer, and worship are vital for one to develop and grow in their identity in Christ.

Fasting

"Go, gather together all the Jews who are in Susa, and fast for me. Do not eat or drink for three days, night or day. I and my attendant will fast as you do. When this is done, I will go to the king, even though it is against the law. And if I perish, I perish" (Esther 4:16).

Fasting involves denying the flesh of food for a specific amount of time. By denying your flesh, your spiritual senses are heightened, and you will find yourself becoming more spiritually in-tune to recognizing God's voice and learning to be obedient to what He has entrusted you with. Over time, variations of spiritual fasting have occurred. Some deny their flesh meat, sweets, or favorite types of food or beverage. Others, especially if you have been diagnosed with a medical condition that requires you to maintain daily consistent meals, may deny the flesh of engaging in certain desired activities for a specific time frame.

For example, I fasted from engaging in social media for three weeks. And when I say fasted, I am referring to not posting, not reading posts, not responding to notifications, not following groups or pages, not reading or commenting on comments, and not watching videos. I have always been a proponent of fasting as a way to connect with God on a deeper level when I am seeking His guidance on a situation, need to focus, and when I do not feel that I hear His voice otherwise. In December 2018, as I did towards the end of every year, I needed to partake in a spiritual fast to prepare for the next season and the following year. I needed to request God's guidance on prioritizing my life. God placed several ideas on my heart in recent years, and once school ended, I was overwhelmed with which avenue to pursue, and most importantly, which venture to pursue first. I found myself scrolling the news feed every chance I got, including breaks at work or at night before falling asleep because it was a mindless activity and allowed my mind to unwind from stressful days. I enjoyed and continue to enjoy watching videos and joining webinars on social media focusing on entrepreneurship, business, inspiration, and book-writing. I became overwhelmed from watching and listening to various videos and authors daily, and in some cases, several times a day. I noticed how easily influenced I was after every video, so I would find myself completing one step or task from various videos. And I am sure that you know that when you spread yourself thin by doing a tad bit of everything, you are not able to complete any one task with quality. I became anxious that I was not moving fast enough in life. I could no longer discern between my voice and my ideas and God's voice and His vision for my life. I needed to fast social media to re-focus. My fast began the day after Christmas and ended in late January. I would replace the time on social media with prayer, communing with God, and reading the Word. It was during and after my social media fast that I felt more spiritually in-tune. What does this mean or what does this look like? It may present itself differently for each person. For me, God communicates with me through my night dreams, through His Word, confirmation through friends who are believers, and through that small, calm voice in my spirit. As I removed social media from my life, I felt more at ease and less anxious.

God whispered in my spirit and reminded me of His purpose in my life, which was to glorify Him and serve His people. God had shown a vivid image that I must be physically and emotionally present in every task that I engage in, from parenting, to my health, to ministry, to my professional life. God had shown me that I was allowing myself to quietly compete with others instead of running my own race, in my own lane, as God had called each of us to do. With that said, God whispered that social media should be used in the following ways, especially when you are a believer: to glorify God and serve His children. It is an avenue to connect with people who God has called to you to connect with, may it be family, friends, people whom God has called you to mentor, and individuals whom you are called to partner with for a God-cause or purpose. I believe that we are called to live a life of transparency, not perfection, so knowing that we are called to be sanctified or set apart, we are to live by example, set the example, as Titus two women (read the book of Titus chapter two). Social media should not be a place to air our disputes or disgust and dislikes with others, instead, bring your concern to that individual after prayer and with godly guidance. Social media should not be a place of gossip, but a place to encourage, empower, and love each other to life. As I slowly began transitioning back into the world of social media, God revealed that the words that would lead my 2019 were: Present, Intentional, and Impactful. I now limit my social media time to checking my notifications once every two days or so. I now post once every week to two weeks, and when I choose to post, my comments should be to encourage, inform, uplift, and empower through applying Scriptures, articles, and personal life lessons. So when you fast, remember to replace that time of the fasted activity with prayer, reading the Bible, and communing with God. In this, you will begin to develop your identity in Christ. And, side note, if you are following someone who is spewing negativity on their page, come from among them and surround yourself with people who will speak into your spirit-that one was for free!

Journaling

"Have you not known? Have you not heard? The Lord is the everlasting God, the Creator of the ends of the earth. He does not faint or grow weary; His understanding is unsearchable. He gives power to the faint, and to him who has no might He increases strength" (Isaiah 40:28-29).

As it has been suggested with your reading of this book, journaling is a powerful tool to allow the issues of the heart to find its way onto paper. Journaling involves you writing your thoughts, questions, emotions, and God-moments down. There is no need for terms to be politically-correct, or to have proper punctuation and grammar. I would suggest having a specific notebook or book as your journal with an inspirational phrase, word, quote, or Scripture to motivate you through this process, in addition to the accompanying workbook. The joy in journaling is to trust the process. It provides an opportunity for you to be vulnerable (only between you and God), observe patterns that come about in your writing, possibly note distorted or uncomfortable thoughts, emotions or behaviors, and begin formulating a plan to remove those negative things in life to make way for healing and restoration. Journaling takes many different forms with writing schedules, the types of journals you have, and even the number of journals you may prefer. You may choose to have a notebook next to you as you read the Bible and simultaneously write whatever freely comes to heart and mind. You may choose to journal after you read the Bible or book that you prefer to read. Others may keep a dream journal, as I do, used to document your night dreams. Some may prefer to journal first thing in the morning, mid-day, during work breaks, or before falling asleep for the night. The important concept to grasp is that journaling may be as structured or as flexible as you prefer; thus, it should not be an arduous task and should not evoke any overwhelming emotions. You may find a sense of peace, revelation, healing, and restoration through the journaling process paving the way for your identity in Christ to be developed.

Prayer

"Come near to God, and He will come near to you. Cleanse your hands, you sinners, and purify your hearts, you double-minded" (James 4:8).

As believers in Christ, your prayer life is essential in establishing and developing your identity in Christ, beloved. Some feel that there is a distinction between prayer and conversation with God, while others do not and believe that the two are one in the same. I will not answer this question for you, but ask yourself, where do you stand on this spectrum? Most importantly, my hope is that you know that prayer involves having intimacy with God. Your prayer life involves developing a relationship with God, and similar to journaling and fasting, allows you to become spiritually in-tune with the One who created you. When fully engaged in prayer, it becomes a two-way communication when both speak and listen. Oftentimes, we hold misconceptions about prayer, such as we must use certain words such as thees and thous, or structured and formal versus informal and flexible. When you come to our heavenly Father, come to Him with respect and in love and adoration. Come to the Father with your heart and in a position of vulnerability, surrender, and in expectation. He may not respond how and when *you feel* that God should, but He will respond in the avenue that He sees best and within His timing. Some prefer to set time aside, such as in the morning when you first wake up, or prior to falling asleep in the evening. Yes, it is important to make your prayer time with God the highest priority, but remember that it is encouraged to have conversations with our Father throughout the day, and to seek His guidance in all decisions, regardless of how big or small you may feel that the decision is. I know it feels easier, at times, to consult with friends and family first regarding situations and decisions, but I challenge you to try something! The next time you have a decision to make, hold on before seeking the guidance of others. Go to your heavenly Father and seek His wisdom. It is life-changing!

I know I may have lost you and you are overcome with a barrage of questions, possibly, such as: *How do I talk to God? How do I hear His voice? What am I listening for? Will others think I'm crazy if I say that I talk to God?* Allow me to explain. God speaks to us in different ways, and how He chooses to speak with us may depend on various factors such as your level of spiritual maturity, your season in life, and your ability to hear or willingness to hear His voice. For instance, I hear God through a word of spiritual advice from others, reading the Bible, God's peaceful whispers in heart, and night dreams. I remember some years ago, I was in a "busy" season in my life, not much different from this point in my life, now that I laughingly think about it, and I had a dream, and when I awoke, I went to God in prayer about the meaning of the dream. God said, "I come to you in your dreams because you're too busy to listen to me any other time." Oh, yes, did you feel that reprimand? I sure did, and I understood what my heavenly Father meant as I had become so preoccupied with life that I missed out on developing intimacy with the One who created me. That statement was not to punish me, but to lovingly correct me, and led me to have a repenting heart. God continues to come to me in my dreams, but now the underlying message of my dreams are to warn me, free me, and guide me. Perhaps God speaks to you or answers your prayer through an encouraging word, confirmation, or advice from someone, such as a pastor, a close friend, or someone who you may value. Now, there's a caveat here. Be mindful of whom you allow to speak into your life and who you allow to pray for you, with you, and over you and your loved ones because not everyone prays to the same God as you. I'll share a recent experience.

A few of the ladies from the single mothers' ministry and I went on a family day trip. I stepped away with the kids and walked along the beach while the moms had time to chat alone. As I was walking, this woman, who appeared less than genuine, said, "Miss, I see an aura about you. You are glowing. I see many good things in your future. Let me share with you about your future. Let me pray with you." I graciously smiled and said, "No!" The look on her face led me to believe that she felt insulted by my response. So she continued, "Please, let me pray with you and tell you what I see. Let me see your hands." I maintained my "no" stance, said thank you, and grabbed one of the children with my right hand, and began walking away, while my teen on my left followed suit. The lady attempted to "pray" for me as we walked on by saying, "You don't want me to pray for you. How do you not want me to pray for you?" I stopped, and while looking at her, with a smile on my face, kindly said, "Thank you, but no thank you." She looked puzzled and irritated as we walked away. I immediately turned to my son and my friend's daughter and shared the following lessons: 1) never allow *just* anyone to pray for you, with you, over you, or lay hands on you, 2) discern, 3) allow the Holy Spirit to guide you on what to say and how to say it; and 4) stand firm in what the Holy Spirit has called you to do." I did not know the woman; thus, I was not aware of whom she served, her spiritual walk, and her intent. When I was not as confident in my relationship with Christ, I was open to anyone and everyone "praying" for me who said they had a word from the Lord for me. We must be mindful, as opening this door to anyone and everyone leaves us spiritually susceptible to ungodly forces and the possibility of becoming spiritually depleted.

"Dear friends, do not believe every spirit, but test the spirits to see whether they are from God, because many false prophets have gone out into the world" (1 John 4:1).

We will get into this in chapter eight, as we will be discussing on hearing the voice of God and obedience, but in the meantime, be mindful of who you allow to pray with you, for you, and over you. Amen.

Worship

"Bless the Lord, O my soul,
And all that is within me,
Bless His holy name!
Bless the Lord, O my soul,
And forget not all His benefits,
Who forgives all your iniquity,
Who heals all your diseases,
Who redeems your life from the pit,
Who crowns you with steadfast love and mercy,
Who satisfies you with good

So that your youth is renewed like the eagle's" (Psalm 103).

So, beloved, how do you worship? Do you worship with your hands raised when the choir sings your favorite hymn? Do you worship in your quiet time with God, bowed down with knees on the floor, hands outstretched, and head bowed down? Perhaps you outpour in words of praise and thanksgiving while in your car driving up to your favorite mountain spot? The truth is that all these are perfect. Worship is the act of the expression of our love, adoration, respect, and honor to God. This expression may come in different forms, both formal and informal, individually or collectively. It may include music or not. Worship may involve verbal and or physical expression of our adoration for our Heavenly Father. Worship is not only in what we say, but how we say it. Worship is our spiritual walk. We may worship God in what we do and in how we do it, providing that it is glorifying God. Being in a place of worship will strengthen your identity in Christ by allowing you to be vulnerable and receptive to not only hear God's voice, but be obedient to Him.

Practical Application

So, what does this look like? I am glad you asked! In the following exercise, you will be asked to apply this concept within your life. In your notebook and workbook, board, or computer, draw two separate lines, from the top of the page to the bottom, creating three columns. In column A, write down all the various roles that you play. Again, role is a position that you play in relation to others. For instance, if you were once married, your relationship to your former spouse was as a wife. As you are completing this task, think of the roles you play in every realm, such as personal (nuclear and extended family, children's school), community in which you live, work life, school, ministry, globally, etc. You should have an extensive list. In column B, write down what the Bible says about you and identity, more specifically focusing on words, phrases, titles that the Bible uses to describe you, and how God sees you or refers to you as. How should you go about completing this task? You may ask, "How do I begin knowing what the Bible says about me?" You may start off by opening your Bible, and if you're like me, I enjoy actually feeling the pages of the Bible through my fingers, writing in it, making notes, and highlighting as I read and study. Whether it is through the hard copy of God's text or a Bible app on your phone, locate the concordance. The concordance is a separate section usually located in the back of the Bible with an alphabetical listing of words used in the Bible text and provides Scriptures that mention that word or phrase. For instance, when looking for Scriptures that describe who you are in God's eyes, look up such words: *ability, able, ambassador, anoint, beautiful, Christ,* and *image*, to name a few. If you do not have a printed Bible, please refer to the internet and locate Scriptures on identity. Yes, we must lead with a heart of caution and discern what results are pulled up, but the hope is for you to have some understanding of biblical principles, how to feel comfortable reading, researching, and studying the Bible, no matter where you are on your spiritual journey. In column C, write down Scriptures that speak specifically to your identity in Christ, so you may refer to them as often as needed. It is okay to feel somewhat challenged by this task as it is in your moments of challenge where growth takes its most beautiful form. Now, let us shift gears and explore your relationship with Christ in chapter two, but before we do, allow some time to review the following Scriptures that relate to your identity in Christ.

My hope for you as we conclude this chapter on developing a solid identity in Christ through prayer, journaling, and fasting, is that you understand the distinction between identity and the roles we play. The first step in the process of achieving harmony is understanding how your relationship with Christ impacts every role we play and every area in our lives, from our God-designed purpose, parenting, community, dating and courtship, and overall well-being. Let's turn to what the Word says about identity, and as you read the following Scriptures, meditate on them, study and cross reference, and ask how you may apply them to your life.

Applicable Scriptures

"And to put on the new self, created after the likeness of God in true righteousness and holiness" (Ephesians 4:24).

"Therefore, if anyone is in Christ, he is a new creation. The old has passed away; behold, the new has come" (2 Corinthians 5:17).

"But you are a chosen race, a royal priesthood, a hold nation, a people for His own possession, that you may proclaim the excellencies of Him who called you out of darkness into His marvelous light" (1 Peter 2:9).

"For in Christ Jesus you are all sons of God, through faith" (Galatians 3:26).

"But to all who did receive Him, who believed in His name, He gave the right to become children of God" (John 1:12).

"And if children, then heirs- heirs of God and fellow heirs with Christ, provided we suffer with Him in order that we may also be glorified with Him" (Romans 8:17).

"No longer do I call you servants, for the servant does not know what his master is doing; but I have called you friends, for all that I have heard from my Father I have made known to you" (John 15:15).

Prayer

My prayer for the lovely one reading this chapter is that she comes to know You, God, and may her connection with You grow deeper and deeper as each day passes. God, as Your daughter enters this new season of change and growth, may she open herself, her heart to You. May she enter a place of vulnerability with You alone, and surrender her hopes, cares, and fears to You. May she relinquish all control, lift her hands up in praise to You, and bow down at Your feet. May she be like the woman who strived with all of her last might to touch the hem of Your cloak to be in Your presence, to be healed and restored by You, so that she is open to God's revelation. May she open her heart and allow You in, and receive what You have for her. Through commune with You, she will come to know and embrace that she is a mighty warrior of God. She is an agent of godly change, a Proverbs 31 woman, an ambassador of Christ, made in Your image and bought with the most magnificent price. She is a daughter of the Most High God, she is royal priesthood, and is more precious than rubies. She is a King's kid, and we bind all things and all people who come against You, trying to block this woman of God from knowing who she is in You. In Jesus' name, we pray, amen.

Chapter 2

What Have I Been Created For?

"For we are God's masterpiece, created to do good works which God pre-pared in advance for us to do" (Ephesians 2:10).

WHAT IS YOUR GOD-DESIGNED PURPOSE?

That's a loaded question, I know, but it is an important question in moving forward in both your spiritual journey and in the physical realm. Women play an integral role in the body of Christ. If only we knew this, understood it, and embraced this God-truth. I am reminded of the following Scripture:

> *"Just as a body, though one, has many parts, but all its many parts form one body, so it is Christ"* (1 Corinthians 12:12).

The enemy knows that we, as women, are powerful tools as we are the vessels through which life is birthed. So with this knowledge, the devil attempts with his many schemes and tactics to kill, steal, and destroy seeds that God has placed in our spirit. If the devil can keep you from walking in and serving in God's purpose, then he is pleased, and he has succeeded. With this said, the devil does his best to get into our minds, to get into our thoughts, and place and grow seeds of doubt.

Is it that thought of opening a business? Perhaps you have thought about writing a book or going back to school. And just as quickly as those thoughts "popped" into your head, it was soon followed by, "Are you serious? You can't write a book. You don't know how. A business? That takes too much money." Maybe it is, "Going back to school...at my age. Who am I kidding? My time is done." Those words may come in your personal thoughts or through a family member or a "friend." Perhaps those negative emotions of yourself emerged from childhood when you were told that you were not good enough. Perhaps they are not thoughts of insufficiency, but of competition and jealousy when you see others doing what you feel you have been called to do. I bind those thoughts, emotions, and feelings in the name of Jesus. They do not have power over you nor who you have been called to be. It is important to distinguish among God's voice, the devil's voice, and your own. Please know that whether it is a discussion on your purpose or any other topic, know that the voice of God and His instruction is to encourage you, empower you, restore you, heal you, guide you, correct you, and will never be words that harm you, tear you down, or create confusion or doubt, beloved.

God created women as social creatures to be in connection with one another meant to empower each other, support one another, and partner with and collaborate with each other as sisters. We were not meant to do life alone. With this said, know that God has created each of us with a specific purpose (individually) meant to fulfill a part of the collective purpose as the body of Christ. You have been bought with a price and called for such a time as this. Yes, I said, "called." There is a calling on your life, sweet one! God created you with a specific purpose, a God-calling, and although you may feel that others are performing similar purposes, God knows that the purpose He has for you has been intentionally designed and tailored for you to execute. No longer walk in a mindset of lack or a mindset of comparison, but walk in a mindset of God-confidence, knowing that God innately gave you what you needed and developed your character through life experiences to walk firmly and boldly in His purpose.

Purpose, calling, vision, and mission all encompass the second step in this process of attaining harmony in life as a single mother. A part of knowing who you are in Christ-it is through your identity in Christ and your relationship with Him-that you open the door to understanding your God-designed purpose. When one knows and embraces what they have been created on this earth to do, it brings synchrony into their lives. It is knowing that our harmony is tied to our purpose. So now, let us get into what purpose, calling, vision, and mission look like.

Purpose

In October 2016, God began to pour out the curriculum that I was to apply to the single mothers' ministry that I was facilitating. At the time, I was in my last semester of coursework before the doctoral dissertation phase began. I was working in a position that was stressful and oftentimes left me in tears some nights, feeling hopeless, helpless, and unsure of who I was, where I was going, and how to move forward. I began to seek God's voice to guide me in a season of what felt like chaos and confusion. God began to whisper the words, *"transition, preparation."* What did this mean? For some time, I thought God was transitioning me into another area of the single mothers' ministry outside of the church. As days turned into weeks, God began to reveal His heart to me and took me on a journey of *purpose-finding* and *call-seeking*. God took me to the Book of Esther, which became one of my favorites in the Bible. He began to unveil purpose, the meaning of purpose, collective purpose, and my individual God-designed and God-given purpose and calling.

God, in His glory and amazement, may not show you the entire picture or stairwell, but show you just what you need when you need it, step by step. And the step that I was on was gaining clarity on the term *transition*. I was not shown the curriculum right away. As a matter of fact, the first step instructed was for me to read the Book of Esther again. As I delved into this book as though I had never read it, my eyes were seeing the words as though it was the first time, and my heart was receptive like a fresh new love. He divided the book into sections for me, and random questions would emerge, such as, what was Esther's purpose? What was her calling? Was there a difference between purpose and calling? How did that translate into my life? Even more importantly, how did that translate into the lives of the women God called me to serve? What were distractions to our purpose? What is the importance of timing when moving in your purpose? God reminded me of what He spoke into my spirit years before, *"What I allow you to do will be used to glorify Me (God) and serve My (God's) people."*

God disclosed that He was preparing me for transition and preparing me for the role of leadership in a different capacity. I did not understand what this meant until now, years later. God whispered in my spirit that He was going to take me on this journey because He needed to prepare me for the next season in life. So I asked, "God, is this a journey for me alone or am I to walk this journey with the mothers of the single moms' ministry that I facilitated?" Instantly, I knew it was a life-changing experience, not only for myself, the mothers of the single moms' ministry, but for women around the world. And here we are!

My Purpose-Defining Moment

Allow me to share more specifically how God boldly revealed my purpose and calling and how He spoke to my heart. It began in 2009 as it was less than one year after I gave my life to Christ. My son was six. I began attending the church that is now my home church. I immersed myself into the Word, the sword, day and night, learning more and more, speaking in my heavenly language, and every time the church doors were open, best believe that my son and I were there. My son was attending private school, and I was allowing what I believed in my heart to be manifested in our lives as believers from the inside out. Do not be mistaken, flaws were and continue to be present, so there is no perfection here, but we must continue to develop a Christlike image daily, allowing less and less of ourselves to conform to the ways of this world, but allowing ourselves to be transformed by the renewing of our minds. I had graduated a few months before with my master's degree in counseling psychology, and was a social worker, providing services for older individuals with developmental disabilities. One evening, I was heading to my son's school on the I-10 (for my West Coast folks), and I began having a conversation with my heavenly Father. I knew in my spirit that there was more that God called me to do, live, and be a part of. God had shown me pieces of the puzzle before, but I was my biggest critic, always professing that "I wasn't ready." So while driving, I asked God, "So God, now what?" I began to share my heart with God. You may ask, "Why? He already knows our hearts." As the Word says,

"Do not be anxious about anything, but in every situation, by prayer and petition, with thanksgiving, present your requests to God. And the peace of God, which transcends all understanding, will guard your hearts and your minds in Christ Jesus" (Philippians 4:6-7).

I was seeking God's wisdom and guidance on the next chapter in life as the Bible proclaims, "Ask, and it will be given to you; seek, and you will find; knock, and it will be opened to you. For everyone who asks receives, and he who seeks finds, and to him who knocks it will be opened" (Matthew 7:7-8).

As my conversation continued with God, I shared that the thought of returning to school for my doctorate had crossed my mind a few times prior to this conversation, but I was uncertain whether it was the right move, whether it was what God desired of me, or whether it was the right time with raising a young child on my own. I heard God, in my spirit, ask, "How will you use this doctorate?" Stunned, perhaps at the realization that God was speaking so clearly to me at all or at the question itself, I stumbled to find the words, and before I could utter a response, I heard, "I will not allow you to pursue your doctorate unless you will use it to glorify Me (God) and serve My (God) people." With tears welling up, and a humble heart, I graciously said, "Yes, Lord. I understand." I knew that my purpose involved having my doctorate.

Now, you will hear, and yes, I heard from others, God can use who He deems fit to carry on His message. Receiving a formal education, certain credentials, degrees in specific fields, allow access, opportunities, and certain doors that may not otherwise be opened. For instance, certain positions, such as a licensed clinical psychologist, is afforded to those who have a minimum of a doctorate degree, certain amount of clinical training hours, and requires certain exams for licensure. No matter how much one wishes to be a licensed clinical psychologist, you must pursue and receive your doctorate degree to even be considered to enter this position. At the time of this conversation, I did not know my God-designed and God-given purpose, or even my calling for that matter; however, I knew that God was preparing me by allowing me to pursue an advanced degree to fulfill my purpose because it was going to allow me access through opportunities that I would not have had access to otherwise. Five years later, after becoming a homeowner, advancing professionally, and continuing to raise my son, I entered my doctoral program. And this conversation with God in 2009 has kept me humble and focused in my most challenging moments over the years.

Purpose-Finding Journey

So, when you think of purpose, what comes to mind for you? Do such terms as passion, calling, anointing, and intentionality spring up? It involves the world's age-old question: Why am I here? People have different perspectives on how to arrive at a response. When I speak of purpose, I am referring to how God spoke it to me, "God-given and God-designed." It is the task and the life that God has created you for. You may not know it as of yet, but let's begin this journey together as you find your path to knowing. There is a distinction between collective purpose and individual purpose, who some may consider as one's *calling*, which we will get into in a little bit. Collectively as God's children, we are called to edify the church, be a vessel for God's light to shine through, encourage and lovingly guide people to Christ, and ultimately in everything that we engage in, through living a life of salvation, glorify God and serve His children as He has called us to. Consider and study the following biblical passages:

> *"From whom the whole body, joined and held together by every joint with which it is equipped, when each part is working properly, makes the body grow so that it builds itself up in love"* (1 Corinthians 3:9).

> *"And we urge you brothers, admonish the idle, encourage the fainthearted, help the weak, be patient with them all. See that no one repays anyone evil for evil, but always seek to do good to one another and to everyone. Rejoice always, pray without ceasing,*

*give thanks in all circumstances: for this is the will
of God in Christ Jesus for you"* (1 Thessalonians 5:14)

How about this one?

> *"For just as the body is one and has many members,
> and all the members of the body, though many, are
> one body, so it is with Christ For in one Spirit we were
> all baptized into one body- Jews or Greeks, slaves or
> free- and all were made to drink of one Spirit. For the
> body does not consist of one member but of many.
> If the foot should say, "Because I am not a hand, I
> do not belong to the body," that would not make it
> any less a part of the body. And if the ear should say,
> "Because I am not an eye, I do not belong to the body,
> "that would not make it any less a part of the body"*
> (Corinthians 12:12).

> *"For as in one body we have many members, and
> the members do not all have the same function,
> so we, though many, are many, are one body in
> Christ, and individually members one in another"*
> (Romans 12:4-5).

As we speak to individual God-given and God-designed purpose, you may ask, how do you begin to explore your purpose?
Has God revealed it to you? Are you receptive? It is first helpful to
engage in self-reflection, where you begin to take self-inventory
on your passion, your primary interests, talents, natural and spiritual gifts, skillset, and those "giftings" that come instinctively to
you. You know, the task or items that although may require time
and hard work, are the very things that you enjoy doing in your
spare time, or if you currently are employed providing those

giftings, they are the areas that you would engage in whether you received monetary compensation or not. I heard a well-known actor refer to passion as "that itch." Yes, it is that thing that you would be doing, whether anyone else was watching and whether you got paid for it or not. What about those areas that you may not necessarily enjoy, but feel a strong yearning towards, such as working with a particular population or participate, initiate, or partner with others on a project (whether one-time or ongoing)? It would be strongly encouraged to attend a "spiritual gifts" class at your home church or take a reputable and biblically-based spiritual gifting test online to pinpoint your areas of giftings. The class or online assessment should provide you your three most prominent gifts; and further offer areas where your spiritual gifts would be most beneficial, either at your church, more specifically, or in general, when working in the community. Consider these areas as you explore your passions and purpose.

Calling

This is a popular term applied within circles of faith. What are your thoughts about calling? How would you define a calling or being called? Is purpose and calling the same? Different? Is one considered superior to the other? Do you feel called to a particular area or to serve a certain demographic? Some individuals define purpose as a collective term meant to serve the purpose of serving others and calling as more tailored to the individual based on their gifts and talents. Let us take the following Scripture:

> "And we know that in all things God works for the
> good of those who love Him, who have been called
> according to His purpose. For those God foreknew

He also predestined to be conformed to the image of His Son, that He might be the firstborn among many brothers and sisters And those He predestined, He also called; those He called, He also justified, those He justified, He also glorified" (Romans 8:28-30).

So a feeling of being called may be described as a yearning, inner gravitational pull towards a particular area, population, or work in the sense of mission. A God-calling, as I refer to it, is specific to you, and God prepares you for such. The question becomes, how receptive are you to that calling, followed by, will you answer the calling that has been God-placed on your life? You oftentimes hear of individuals in positions of spiritual authority describe a period of time when they felt God call them to a particular ministry such as being a pastor. How will your calling impact those of your immediate circle and family?

Vision

Separate from purpose and calling, it is important to have vision. What is vision, or perhaps what is the distinction between vision and purpose? Vision is the inspiration behind your purpose. It is what guides you to step into walking into your purpose. It inspires you, fuels you, moves you to the change that you want to see. Perhaps you want to open a business, or God has instructed you to do so; have you explored the vision of this desire? Where do you see your business in five, ten, thirty years from this moment, and what impact do you expect the business to have? What change do you want to see? Perhaps you desire to open a program for young men ages 15 to 25 in your city that is geared towards providing job training. For example, you conducted qualitative research on the challenges that males of this population encounter, such as crime, violence, gang activity, and high levels of incarceration. After exploring the specific challenges for this demographic and services and programs that may be in place in your city, you have determined that there is a gap, where not all of these challenges are addressed. One's vision for the said business may be to ensure that every male in this demographic within your city gains meaningful employment within the next ten years. Another vision may be that every male be professionally prepared to gain meaningful employment within the next five years. For someone with the desire to open a homeless shelter for women, their vision may fall along the line of ensuring that every woman has a warm and clean bed to safely sleep in every night. Ask yourself, what is the change that you want to see as a result of walking in your purpose and living in your calling?

Mission

In our society, mission is a commonly used word, and this is especially true among the nonprofit sector. I often refer to mission as the link or bridge between one's purpose and their vision. Purpose and calling involves living the life God has called you to live, serving His children as He has called you to serve them, and glorifying Him in the process. Vision is the inspiration that has led you to live and walk in your purpose meant to make an impact in the lives of others. Mission is the link between what you have been divinely created to do and the inspiration that fuels it. Mission is how the purpose and vision are manifested. It involves the tangible items. For instance, let us say that you want to open an organization that is geared towards providing support, resources, and education to families of individuals living with a clinical mental illness. Perhaps you took a self-assessment years ago and found that your spiritual gifts involve exhortation, mercy, and teaching. Through your personal, professional, academic, and spiritual journey, you have developed a strong skillset in these areas. God revealed to you that your God-designed and God-given purpose was to provide support and empowerment for the loved ones of individuals who are living with mental illness. God revealed to you that the vision behind your purpose of supporting those family members is to see every family member educated about mental illness and empowered. So your mission is to express how the vision is manifested in the tangible realm. Your purpose is to support loved ones of those living with mental illness. Your vision is to see every family member educated about mental illness and be empowered. Your mission is to fulfill your vision of education and empowerment through writing books, holding workshops and conferences, and conducting support groups within the community geared towards defining mental illness, education on mental illness, and various mental health diagnoses, connecting family members with other individuals with similar experiences, and providing resources.

Approximately three years ago, God gave me a night dream. When I refer to a "night dream," I am speaking to the actual act of dreaming and not necessarily a wish or desire in the future. I appeared to be in my forties in the dream as I was slightly older than I am now. I was in a substantially large area that appeared to be an open outdoor parking lot and stands of bleachers in the distance surrounding the parking lot as though it were a car race track. A younger man was walking with me. There were thousands of women of all ages, various ethnicities, and walks of life. They were standing, walking, and lying down on gurneys in tents throughout the open space. Each woman, child, and family represented had a desire to be prayed for and prayed with. God revealed that He was using me as a vessel, and I would pray for each person. Before the individuals spoke, I would place my hands over their hands, and God would give me God-vision of where that individual was in their life spiritually, the challenges and trials they endured, and how and what I specifically needed to pray for as I prayed with them. As I began walking the premises, my eyes rested upon an African American family of three, an older woman who laid on a gurney, her daughter in her forties who stood to the left of her, and the daughter's seven-year-old daughter who was sitting towards the foot of the gurney appearing oblivious to what was taking place. I stood in front of the family; I noticed that they were within a covered tent, one of the thousands that were up that day. It was the kind of tent that you would see at the park when a family was having a barbeque, with the covering on top, a rod holding up each of the four corners, and no coverings on the sides. I walked towards the grandmother. She did not appear physically ill; however, she laid on the gurney coherent and able to advocate for herself. The grandmother said, "I don't trust folks (exploitative)." It was a heart issue as she spoke to unforgiveness, pain, anger, and bitterness. The grandmother, the matriarch of this family, appeared distrusting and proud of her cold, almost heartless approach. I placed my hands over the grandmother's hands, and God began to reveal the challenges and the pain of this woman's past and how that had impacted the daughter. I began to speak what God was showing me. I shared the family's history of incest, molestation, strongholds, pain, and unforgiveness. As these words were spoken, my eyes rested upon the daughter as she began to wail, standing, almost stooping beside her mother (the grandmother), physically confirming that the words that were being revealed to me in the spirit resonated with her. The daughter had lived her life as many of us women do, stoic, unphased to the trials of life, not needing help, and can handle any and everything that comes her way...with a mask that covered the scars, bruises, and pain, the shame and guilt that is not ours to carry. I looked to the oldest of this three-generation family of women and shared that strongholds must be acknowledged and gutted at the root, or the legacy of these spiritual strongholds will attach itself to generations that follow, and I looked to the granddaughter, unaware of the strongholds that she was born into. I began to pray healing, faith, and restoration over the family, binding what was loosed and created over this family; thus, opening the path of forgiveness. When I awoke, God led me to a close friend as God revealed to me that my close friend, who was a mentor and someone I considered a spiritual godmother, had a word from God for me. And that she did, indeed!

I share this dream with you because God revealed to me as He has continued to confirm over the years, what He has instructed me to do, and to whom He has called me to serve. When you listen carefully, beloved, He will reveal to you ever so gently when you trust Him and trust the journey He has called you on.

Practical Application

Several years ago, when I became a born-again Christian, I decided to enroll into several one to four-week classes at my church. One of which was a class geared towards spiritual giftings. This class provided biblical principles, the definition of spiritual gifts, and identified spiritual gifts through a tool for self-inventory of personality traits and areas that one felt naturally inclined to participate in. My spiritual gifts include exhortation, mercy, and discernment. Exhortation is the ability to encourage and empower others. Mercy is the gift of compassion for others. Discernment is the ability to discern or perceive in your spirit, beyond the physical realm, when something does not feel quite right with a situation or someone's character. As a child and well into my teenage years, I had a desire to want to help others, whether it was a situation one was experiencing or physically assisting someone with a task. I was the individual people would gravitate to for advice or suggestions. So it was natural for me to explore professions that involved the opportunity to work with people. I was drawn to the fields of psychology for the counseling aspect, and nursing due to the innate nature of wanting to help others, and then I read that there was an a strong probability that I would need to learn the art of giving vaccines. Yes, the sight of blood and needles leaves me squirming and on the verge of passing out to this day, so I thought, "This may not work for myself or the person on the other end of the needle." When exploring undergraduate majors, I took countless courses in psychology, sociology, women studies, religion, philosophy, ethnic studies, and anthropology because I had this love and desire to learn all that I could about people, how others lived, what their experiences were, how similar and different my life may have been from theirs, and what we may teach each other.

So let us make this more personal and provide you an opportunity to apply what we have discussed into your own life.

As you are exploring your spiritual path, it is imperative that you are on one accord with our Heavenly Father. I hope that by sharing my purpose-finding journey and I how I came to know and understand my calling, you are encouraged to enter and continue on your individual journeys. If you do not know what you have been divinely created to do in this world, please start with a conversation with God and prayer. During your conversation with God, come from a place of surrender, sharing your desires, share your fears, be receptive, and be willing to be still and listen to what God has to reveal to you. During this intimate conversation, delve a step further from not only inquiring about your purpose, but inquiring about your calling and that inner gravitational yearning. Yes, pay attention to that. It would also be a good time to seek pastoral guidance during this time and request for your spiritual circle of influence to keep you in prayer during this period as you seek God's will for your life. Revelation may occur immediately, it may occur over time, you may be led to fast, you may be led to journal, or to kneel and bow in worship and praise. I would suggest reading the following books in the Bible on spiritual giftings so you become familiar with the many gifts that God has bestowed upon you, especially Romans 12:3-8, as it describes prophesying, encouraging, teaching, mercy, giving, serving, and leading. Yes, these are the spiritual gifts in the body of Christ. Additionally, I would suggest exploring your support system and your resources, starting with your home church. Check the church directory and call the office or speak with the pastoral staff, inquiring whether they offer a class or series of classes geared towards defining and exploring your spiritual gifts. If your home church states that they do not have a class geared towards spiritual gifts, please ask for their recommendations. Perhaps they have a resource designed with spiritual gifting self-assessment. Remember to not place a time frame during this time as seeking your purpose and calling is a process and may take days, weeks, months, and even years. Do not allow the word *years* to frighten you as God may reveal the step that you are currently on and gradually introduce a new piece in your purpose finding journey as time progresses.

As your purpose, vision, and calling become clear to you, ask God for confirmation, perhaps through a Word by a close fellow believer, a Scripture, or through a night dream or vision on when to move, how to move, and if and with whom to move with. I would suggest to journal during this time, and be open to the idea of fasting as well. As clarity continues to be revealed, ask God to reveal the mission on how this move is to unfold.

Another practical exercise is to include your family. What I mean by this suggestion is to invite your family to come together as one to discuss the purpose, vision, and mission for your family. For instance, a few months ago, God led me to start the new year by having a conversation with my teenaged son, discussing spiritual gifts, purpose, calling, vision, and mission. My son shared that he did not know his spiritual gifts, but found that he gravitated to serving others with over five years volunteering as a junior leader in the children's ministry and as a mentor for younger Taekwondo students. I introduced him to an online Christian-based self-assessment for adolescents to explore his spiritual gifts. The results confirmed the areas that my son felt a gravitation towards. Through prayer, frequent discussions, seeking pastoral guidance, the self-assessment, and time, my son believes that he has clarity on the area and the demographic that God is directing him to serve. As a mother, I stay in continuous prayer and intercession for my son's spiritual gifts, his life, and his future. One Sunday evening, my son and I pulled out a poster board where I wrote my God-designed purpose, vision, and God-instructed mission, along with a guiding Scripture that God placed in my heart. Likewise, my son wrote the purpose, vision, mission, and guiding Scripture that God revealed to him on the same poster board. On another section of the same poster board, after continuous prayer, we as a family wrote the God-given purpose, vision, and mission that God has laid in our heart, along with a guiding Scripture for our family. This is a suggested exercise for you and your family. Consider framing your family poster or having it laminated and placing in a central location that you and your family would see on a regular basis as a reminder.

And while on the topic, remember to incorporate specific time frames within both your personal mission and family mission of what you hope to accomplish. This is a great time to mention S.M.A.R.T. goals. Have you heard of the term S.M.A.R.T. goals? The concept is reported to be introduced by George Doran in 1981. It involves breaking your mission statement into specific, measurable, attainable, relevant, and timely goals. Do you have a mission statement or know how to create a draft? With the exercise described above, you may use the mission that you created, either individually or with your family, and develop a shortened version to create your guiding statement. The mission statement should have several key components: a brief description and definition of your purpose, reflect your core beliefs, if the statement is for your family or group of individuals, it should speak to the group's action and role collectively, it should allow an opportunity for all members to be involved, describe the target audience, and explains the strategy on *how* you plan to accomplish the mission. As you are developing your mission statement, it should be divided into short term and long term goals. As you write your mission, it should be specific and thorough. When goals are vague, it leads to the possibility of the mission never being fulfilled and opens the door for distraction. It should be measurable, such that it incorporates specific time frames, and as small short term goals are accomplished, it lends to an opportunity for more established goals to be pursued. Your mission statement and general goals should be attainable, relevant, and lastly, timely. The last three emphasizes that it should be structured in a format that makes the goal or mission achievable, the short term goal should be pertaining to the purpose, and be within a timely period. Following the S.M.A.R.T. goals technique allows you to stay focused.

I am hoping, with this chapter, you have come to understand how your purpose, calling, vision, and mission are correlated to achieving harmony in your life. Let us explore Scriptures that apply to what God-designed purpose is revealed in our lives.

Applicable Scriptures

"This is what the Lord says: "When seventy years are completed for Babylon, I will come to you and fulfill my good promise to bring you back to this place. For I know the plans I have for you," declares the Lord, "plans to prosper you and not to harm you, plans to give you hope and a future. Then you will call on me and come and pray to me, and I will listen to you. You will seek Me and find Me when you seek Me with all your heart" (Jeremiah 29:10-13).

"Before I formed you in the womb I knew you; and before you came forth out of the womb I sanctified you, and I ordained you a prophet unto the nations" (Jeremiah 1:5).

Prayer

Heavenly Father, thank you for preparing for me this next season in life. Lord, thank you for creating me for purpose, with purpose, and on purpose. And in the event in which I did not know until this very moment that I was created with godly purpose in mind, thank you for finding me worthy to reveal who I am in You and what You have specifically called me for. Father, make Your vision in my life plain and clear as You have ordered my steps. May I be in a place and space to receive Your revelation. Purge all things that are not of You. Purge all addictions, strongholds, generational curses, relationships, idols, and soul ties from my life, and begin Your work in me, one of healing, of restoration, and transformation. As I mature in You, draw nearer to You, draw nearer to me, as Your Word says, and reveal how I am to move, when I am to move, and who You have called to move into this next season with me. Teach me Your ways, Heavenly Father, and share revelation through Your Word via biblical principles, parables, and

Scripture. May revelation be revealed through visions, dreams, and in the prophetic realm. Give me Your strength to withstand the trials that come my way as distractions to keep me from fulfilling what You have called me to. Remove all fear and anxiety, and may I move in faith every step of this journey, for I am someone's promise, for there are people waiting for me to do what You have called me to. Heavenly Father, I am ready. Your daughter is ready; equip me for the journey ahead. In Jesus' name, we pray, amen and amen.

Chapter 3

Preparation Is Birthed Through Perseverance

"When anxiety was great within me, your consolation brought me joy"
(Psalm 94:19).

HAVE YOU EVER EXPERIENCED A CHALLENGING time when you were not sure what the outcome was going to be or whether you were going to survive through it? When fear gripped you? When depressed feelings contributed to self-isolation, engagement in addictions, such as overeating, alcoholism, or drugs, both recreational and prescribed? When anxious thoughts crowded your mind and the enemy attempted to inundate your spirit with doubt meant to destroy the very essence of you? The truth is that all of us have experienced such trials. And may I whisper another truth to you: this challenging period is only for a moment, a season, a period of time, despite what you think, feel, or how your body responds.

Let us backtrack and review what we have discussed thus far in the last two chapters and how it prepares us as we move forward in this book. We spoke on the importance of understanding the difference between who you are in Christ and the roles that we play in our lives. In this regard, we delved into how prayer, journaling, and fasting can be vital tools in strengthening our relationship with Christ and ultimately develop our character and identity in Christ. Next, we jumped into understanding our God-designed and God-given purpose and how knowing this God truth can prepare us in identifying God's mission and vision in our lives. One important piece in developing the character of God in creating a solid foundation in Christ, identity-strengthening, and purpose-finding is understanding how to recognize trials. And understanding how to persevere through them triumphantly. This is where mindset plays a vital role in learning how to persevere through challenges.

Mindset

All of us experience some form of trials and spiritual warfare. And whether we define an event as spiritual warfare and how we determine the severity of spiritual warfare varies for each person. One's ability to persevere through challenges depends on the mindset. How do you *choose* to perceive a situation? Yes, I use the word *choose* intentionally because it implies that you play a role in determining how you perceive a situation and how you will respond. Will you respond or will you react? And yes, there is a distinction between the two. Do you analyze the situation before making a decision, or do you allow impulse and emotions to take over before you get the facts? Do you tend to see life as a glass half-full or half-empty? Are you an optimist, pessimist, or refer to yourself as a realist? This approach of addressing, evaluating, and changing your mindset stems from the understanding that there is a relationship among thoughts, emotions, and behaviors as suggested in traditional cognitive behavior therapy models. Essentially, it is having an understanding that one's thoughts impact his or her feelings and emotions along with the words one uses to speak about their life and life circumstances. Ultimately, one's thoughts and emotions impact one's behavior. Take for instance the following Scripture:

"Do not be conformed to this world, but be transformed by the renewal of your mind, that by testing you may discern what is the will of God, what is good and acceptable and perfect" (Romans 12:2).

How we perceive a difficult event in our lives and we address it starts with having a sound mindset. Notice in the beginning of the chapter I did not use the term, *obstacle*, but rather trial, challenge, or period because the term *obstacle* implies that it is unstoppable and nonpermeable. Select your words wisely because how you speak and think of the situation and the feelings you allow yourself to experience towards the situation will dictate if, when, how, and how long it takes you to move through it. It is a test of performance. How will you pass this test? What I am speaking of is reframing how you choose to perceive a situation. For instance, a dear friend and I had a conversation about regrets, recently. She said, "I regret doing this," speaking of a particular situation that she felt would have changed the trajectory of her life course. Rather than agree, I chose to offer her a different perspective and a different experience from the one she was having. So I replied, "Do I wish that I would have made different choices in some instances? Oh absolutely. But do I have regrets? No." Why, you may ask? Because those choices, although may not have been ideal, helped to shape and mold me into the woman I am today. So again, it is about perception, paradigm, and the words you choose to describe the experience.

Allow me to ask you this question: what or who influences your thoughts? What is your worldview? Your worldview is the lens in which you see the world. Perhaps you have a biblical worldview that dictates how you perceive the world, how you make your decisions, and how you respond to situations may be based on the Word of God and your relationship with Christ. Perhaps you have a scientific worldview allowing you to see the world in a pragmatic way in black and white, and based on tangible facts and evidence-based. When persevering through a trial, your mindset is your first line of defense as it is how you choose to approach the challenging situation.

As a believer in Christ, your mindset should be set on the things of God. What is your current mental state? How are you feeding it for the better? What are you feeding your mind to change from a negative mindset to one of positivity? And once you have attained a consistent mindset, how you are maintaining it is vital. It is a paradigm shift that is not easy, but is definitely possible. It takes diligence and persistence to choose the lens in which to see the world and make your decisions. This leads us to another important part of perseverance: faith and trusting God in the process.

Trust God in the Process

"Then you will win favor and a good name in the sight of God and man. Trust in the Lord with all your heart and lean not on your own understanding; in all your ways submit to Him, and He will make your paths straight" (Proverbs 3:4-6).

Did I strike a chord with you? Perhaps not. I do not know about you, but faith is an area that I have struggled with. In 2014, the test of faith was evident when I almost lost my home to foreclosure. Six months into my doctoral program, I received a letter from my lender regarding foreclosure proceedings. Now one does not receive a letter of this nature unless you are significantly behind on your mortgage. My expenses had changed with a growing child, additional responsibilities, and all while my wages remained the same. I was paid bi-weekly with my mortgage payment being one full check and part of the subsequent check. This left me with insufficient funds to pay my other expenses monthly. It began with falling behind one month in mortgage. I was no longer paying the mortgage of the current month, but was paying the mortgage of the previous month and it continued this way for some time. This pattern fell into making the decision not to pay the mortgage for the month so that I may catch up on other expenses. To stay current with my other expenses meant to be behind on my mortgage, and to stay current with my mortgage meant to be behind on my other expenses. I could not find balance between my mortgage and my other expenses.

I was private with my affairs. Close friends, family, and men I was formerly romantically involved with began to either offer to donate money or loan money. And other times, I would ask. This pattern of robbing Paul to pay Peter, if you are familiar with that phrase, was using the funds others lent me to pay towards bills, but yet never fully paying off my debts, and only temporarily catching up on bills to fall behind again the following month. This was not a good situation that I allowed myself to slip into. I felt ashamed and guilty to ask others for money, especially from a former boyfriend, one move I would never suggest to anyone. As Proverbs 22:7 says, "The rich rule over the poor, and the borrower is slave to the lender" (NIV).

As time went on, one month of not paying mortgage became two months. At that time, I contacted the lender, informing them that I wanted to make a mortgage payment. I was informed that once you create a pattern of unstable mortgage payment history, as an attempt to assist the homeowner, one mortgage payment was not enough. It was the homeowner's responsibility to make a payment of a mortgage and a half, so essentially, one month's payment and a mortgage payment of the following month to assist the homeowner in catching up. As my jaw dropped while holding the phone, I gasped when the customer service representative continued to say, "Yes, after two months of paying a mortgage and a half payment each, you will be caught up by the third month." With tears in my eyes and a trembling voice, I replied,

"It took me some time to save for one mortgage payment while catching up on my other expenses. This arrangement will cause me to become more behind on my mortgage if I am required to make a payment for a mortgage payment and a half." The representative, although kind, maintained that it was their policy as a strategy for their homeowners to become current. She offered several alternatives and resources, including loan modification. I hung up the phone and worry began to sink in. Faith was the furthest concept from my mind. I began gathering all the documents my lender and other agencies requested. I applied for the loan modification program with my lender, which was a lengthy process. I applied to a nationally well-known home purchase and foreclosure prevention assistance program. I researched several agencies via internet, friends, and my lender. My lender informed me of one program that was geared towards mortgage assistance, loan modification, foreclosure prevention, and refinance. In the midst of this chaos with applying for various programs, my mind was focused on raising my son, working full-time, and hopefully saving my home. My studies suffered from every moment outside of work being directed towards my son and researching and submitting information to stop the foreclosure from happening. This resulted in me failing two doctoral courses. Because I could not afford to pay the amount that my lender was asking in total, it was strongly urged by the lender to no longer make any more mortgage payments because "it would be lost money." Essentially, I was told that it would be up to me, and the customer representative gently suggested that I use the money that I was no longer paying the mortgage to be used towards catching up on all other debts and expenses.

Weeks went by, and one by one, letters began rolling in from the various programs, notifying me that I was denied, including a denial from my loan modification request from my lender. By this point, hope grew faint. One Saturday afternoon, I was cleaning my bedroom floor. Directly across the hallway was my son's bedroom, where I heard my 11-year-old loudly playing with his action figures, not understanding the chaos that his mother was trying to shield him from. I was listening to my favorite Christian radio station. I recall standing up against the wall and sliding into a seated position on the floor while still holding the broom. I began talking to God as I was sitting there, helpless, on the floor. My eyes were dry because I had cried so much about possibly losing my home that no more tears would come. I sat in silence. I was in a place of surrender. My prayer was, "God, I've done all that I know how to do. I don't know what else to do, but give it all to You. I surrender all to You. I surrender this house to You. God, if it is Your will for this house to move into foreclosure, then I know that You have a different plan, a better plan, and I trust You. Lord, I just ask that if this house is meant to no longer be my house, please bless us with a safe alternative, another place we may call our own." I instantly was at peace. It was the type of peace that surpassed all understanding. I stood up and kept sweeping while my son continued to enjoy his play-time. I knew that whichever direction God would have us go, He was going to provide for our every need, and He was going to take care of us.

That Sunday night, I had a dream. In the dream, I was talking to "Michael," who in my dream was the individual I was working with within my lender's company to assist in foreclosure prevention. Michael was the same individual assisting me throughout this process in my real life. In my dream, Michael called me one morning and said, "Ms. Serano, it was approved. You're going to stay in your home." I remember waking up that Monday morning with a smile on my face and whispering, "Gosh, that would be wonderful if that happened in real life." As I reached over to check my phone lying on the bed stand, I noticed that my voicemail light was on, indicating that I had a voice message waiting for me. I saw that Michael had called while I was asleep. Not thinking anything more of the call, I knew that I would call him while en route to my first appointment for work. I, indeed, called Michael while en route; however, he did not pick up, so I decided to call later that morning before my next appointment. Again, an hour later, I called Michael and was able to speak with him immediately. He said, "Ms. Serano, how are you today?" He went on to say, "I have good news for you. It has been approved!" My response was, "I'm sorry. What?" Michael followed by saying, "The last agency that you applied for approved your application, and they have agreed to pay over $11,000 to bring your mortgage current, effective immediately. You will not be able to refinance or sell your home for 3 years, according to the requirements, but other than that, you will continue to stay in your home." This was during the time when we were legally allowed to drive while speaking on our handheld cell phone. I cried, praising God, and thanked Michael for helping me through the entire process. This occurred on February 11, 2014.

Now, I am sure that you are probably wondering how God turned things around for my doctoral studies. After failing two classes, I was expected to be withdrawn from the program in the following quarter as doctoral students were required to receive a grade of B or above in all courses. I was provided information to appeal my withdrawal and was given a date to appear in front of ten individuals to present my case to return to the program. At the time of my appeals date, I had been enrolled in another course and had passed the course with an A as it was after my home was saved. There I was sitting in front of faculty, student employees, and those in a position to determine my fate in the doctoral program. I shared the source behind my lack of focus, the resolution, how I planned to stay on track, and that I was ready to finish the remainder of my doctoral journey. I sat in silence, watching the dean's next move, and she asked, "What have you learned from this experience?" Wow. Well, I jumped in without hesitation, saying, "I learned that I'm stronger than I thought and that I can push through anything." I sat there proudly, looking for their next response. And then it happened. I was hit with this statement by the department chair, "I was hoping that you would say that you learned the valuable lesson of taking time to tend to self, time to assess the situation." I sat quietly, listening. This is someone whom I valued and whom I continue to view as a spiritual, academic, and professional mentor. She went on to say, "It is knowing yourself. It is knowing when it is okay to take a break for mental clarity. You do not always have to move on a high fast-paced trajectory that sometimes we need to take a break from school or other areas so that we may focus on more important affairs." After the committee members met, I was granted to return to the program. But that conversation struck a chord and lingered with me as I drove home. I realized that I had been living this fast-paced lifestyle, but had not allowed myself time to digest the process of almost losing my home and the emotional rollercoaster of the process. Although I persevered through the experience, I had to ask myself what physical and emotional changes accompanied that journey.

Returning to our initial topic of creating an opportunity for a paradigm shift, shifting your perception of the situation that you view as a challenging period in your life is a vital component in your perseverance journey. The mindset of understanding that this situation that I am currently enduring is impossible is a very different mindset in comparison to the mindset of this situation is developing one's character. Developing the mindset of the latter is a teachable moment and is a vital component in achieving harmony in life. It is a moment for growth and will be used as a tool to teach others in similar situations how to persevere triumphantly. One thought that we must constantly dispute internally is because we may identify as Christian, we believe in

God, or try to live a flawless life and participate in favorable works, that challenges will not come our way. Or that all we have to do is try everything in the natural realm, and everything will work out the way we wanted or anticipated. The truth is there are times even when we try all that we can in the natural, things or situations may not turn out the way we wanted or expected because God's perfect will will ultimately be done. It is vital to trust God in the process. Sometimes, it may not make sense to you why situations have occurred the way they have. The timing may seem irrational. But remember to trust God in the process and allow Him to reveal to you what He has for you, and allow Him to do so within His timing and in His divinely unique way.

Removing Distractions

What is distracting you from moving through this journey, that although challenging, must be traveled to get to the other side? I will speak to this topic more in my next book, but it is vital that you, reading this passage, explore what a distraction is, how to identify the source of the distraction, and how to move through it. Let us define distraction. Distraction is defined as to draw apart, separate, or turn towards a different direction from the source. Another definition is to confound, harass, or keep one mind from focusing on God as the source and placing substantial attention on the cares of the world.

Allow us to explore the famous story told in Luke 10 verses 38-42, of sisters, Martha and Mary. I am sure that you are familiar with the story, and there are various interpretations and lessons that derive from the powerful biblical story. Martha welcomed Jesus into her and Mary's home as Jesus entered the village. Martha was focused on cleaning the home, preparing a meal, and serving because she wanted to make it perfect for Jesus. Mary chose to sit at the feet of Jesus and listen to His teaching. Martha was frustrated when she observed Mary sitting down, listening to Jesus, and expected Mary to assist her in the task of serving. Martha, assumingly called herself telling on Mary to Jesus, with possibly the hope that Jesus may require Mary, to leave Him to assist Martha. Jesus did no such thing as His response to Martha was, "Martha, Martha, you are anxious and troubled about many things, but one thing is necessary. Mary has chosen the good portion, which will not be taken away from her."

Reading this story, you may ask yourself, "But how is this so, I do not understand as Martha was doing a good thing, right? She simply wanted her home to be just right, even more than that, but perfect. He is JESUS, after all. If it were us having a gathering at our home and we were expecting someone of extreme royalty, we may possibly respond the same. But allow us to delve deeper and see it from the eyes of Jesus. Martha was distracted, and although it was a good distraction, nonetheless, it was a distraction drawing her away from the presence of the Lord, drawing her away from the nuggets of wisdom that was being imparted by Jesus. There are opportunities that may come once in a lifetime, and although you are doing something else that is positive, it may not be the route that God directed. Let us bring it close to home. Perhaps you were volunteering at a local church or possibly working as an intern receiving none or little monetary compensation. While there, you receive an invitation for an opportunity to work at a well-known company out of state. This is a great opportunity. In fact, it seems like the logical thing to do. You do not pray about or seek godly wisdom on the decision because, again, it seems like that would be the next logical step. Your worldview based on culture, society, values, and your experience tells you that you would be irrational if you did not take this opportunity. The opportunities for growth, although slow at your current volunteer or intern position, is promising, but your natural heart tells you that the natural progression is to always go after the money. I am not saying that in some circumstances, taking this other opportunity is not right, but what I am saying is to be aware of an opportunity of what seems logical is sometimes guised as a distraction, as in the case of Martha.

Distractions or the process of being drawn away from the focus, especially in this case, focus on God, can take different forms such as a behavior that we may engage in, such as with Martha, people and relationships, situations, and even yourself. Distractions may show itself as an overt distraction, meaning that it is apparent and easily recognized by you that the situation, person, or event is meant to pull you away from the lesson that God is teaching you. Other times, the distraction is more covert or subtle when the distraction seems like the right thing to do or is not inherently a negative thing.

How are you able to identify distractions? The items, situations, people and relationships, or yourself who hinders you from staying focused on God, from staying faithful through the challenging period, or through a situation that does not make sense to you. The spiritual reality is that the devil will use whichever vice in his arsenal to steal, kill, and destroy. But the additional truth to that piece is that we cannot blame all distractions to persevere through trials on the enemy. Perhaps you are your own enemy through not holding your thoughts captive, and perhaps allowing fear, lack of confidence, and low self-esteem, and ultimately, lack of faith to keep you from persevering through. Perhaps it is relationships or associations with people who distract you from persevering through the journey and hindering you from focusing on God in this challenging season.

Understand the difference between what or who is pulling you from moving through the challenge and when a situation is an opportunity meant to grow you through it. As you move through the trial, know the difference between how God's spirit in you is guiding you versus the emotions that you feel because they are vastly different. As you persevere through challenging moments in your life, do you notice patterns of relationships, situations, or feelings that are evoked that you know are not of God? Here is a tip. When a situation, a relationship, a thought, or a behavior goes against God and His Word, this is an indication that it is meant as a distraction to steal, kill, and destroy. Another indication of a distraction, among other concerns, is when the situation or decision leaves you confused, chaotic, and not at peace. God is not a God of confusion or chaos, but one of decency and order. God is never, and notice that I use an absolute term, *never* going to make you feel uncertain as He brings clarity, comfort, wisdom, and guidance when we seek Him.

When Perseverance Means Standing Alone

Is it that cousin who says, "Girl, you have been having problem after problem while trying to finish that degree. What should have taken you two years is taking three years, and you are still not done. You need to let that go." Or that friend who is not happy with their job, so as you persevere through the struggling moments of your job, that friend displaces their ill feelings from their job onto you. Yet, you feel something in your spirit telling you not to give up yet.

I recall some years ago, I was invited to speak at an engagement. I had several previous speaking engagements; however, this engagement was different because I was asked to speak to a demographic whom I had not met prior. This event was for approximately 50 women. During this season, I was frantically working on the final stage of my doctoral program while working full time, living the mom-of-a-teenager life, and being involved in ministry. A woman who I met through work invited me to speak after several hours of chatting. I was excited, yet nervous because I knew that God was calling me to a higher place, which led to a higher level of responsibility. As those of you involved in leadership positions are aware, being called to a higher level of responsibility means a higher level of account-ability as you are being called to speak into the lives of others. Your voice, your spirit, your heart, your voice may be used to either empower and uplift or destroy and hinder. I remember saying yes, but needing time to pray and fast about this level of responsibility and accountability. I kept this engagement quiet, only revealing to two close friends who were a part of my godly circle of influence. They immediately began praying for the event to run smoothly. They also prayed for the ladies who were to attend, for the speakers to speak a word given by God, and for me to allow God to use me as a vessel on that day. When almost two months from the event, I recall sharing my excitement.

During this time, a pastor friend was editing her first book in which she had weekly get-togethers at her family home for a small group of us ladies to read, discuss, and critique the writing of the book. I was feeling insecure about sharing this event to everyone. Perhaps it was not a big deal, and fear had developed. I pushed past the fear and decided to send the invite to the ladies of the weekly get-togethers, including my pastor friend. Immediately, texts started to come in one after the other of several ladies making arrangements to drive the hour and a half to attend. These ladies were not women who I would see often outside of the weekly get-togethers for book critique, but it warmed my heart.

God breathed a word in my spirit, "I'm (God) elevating your circle of influence." As fear tried to creep in during the days leading up to the event, I recall receiving a heartfelt text from my pastor friend and several other family and friends who shared the importance of persevering through the distractions of fear, through the trials because women were going to be at that event to hear a word, and I needed to be equipped to allow God to use me as a vessel for which His Word was coming through at that moment.

Your circle of influence is crucial as you move through and persevere through the trials of life. There are moments when you feel that you are alone on this journey. These are the most difficult moments because God created us to be in connection with each other and not do life alone. Those periods of feeling alone are just that; moments, temporary moments of time! There are times when God will allow you to be isolated so that you may focus on Him, not be distracted, but be encouraged and equipped to address and cope with situations that come your way. I have never been one of quantity, but a person of quality. I value quality friendships and sisterhoods, those few friends who will pray with you and for you, and likewise, you do for them. There is power when two or more agree in His name. Your circle of influence should not be a distraction, but should be there to encourage you, uplift you, and likewise, you being there for them in the same capacity as true friendship and sisterhood is a two-way street, where both parties are giving and receiving in the friendship. This is especially true when persevering through the challenges of life.

Dear one, I know that it is challenging at times to remain focused on God's plan, to remain focused on His voice, and His heart. It is during these challenges entering your life as a person, naysayers, a situation, or your own thoughts and emotions, that the enemy will use to hold you captive. If the enemy can keep and entertain your mind, the battle has been won. The enemy will distract you from persevering through a difficult season in your life. Remember that you have the victory, and through any cost, you must trust God through this journey.

Answered Prayers Come Through Perseverance

I gave my life to Christ on July 27, 2008, the day after my birthday. My son and I were living on the first floor of an apartment located in the back of the complex, which was not the safest location. This area was infested with drugs, had active gang activity, and my apartment was burglarized about one year prior. In 2009, my son and I were arriving home one evening. As I drove onto the street that my apartment was located on, I noticed young men standing in a circle. One young man was wearing a white t-shirt. He stood in the middle while 6-9 young men in black t-shirts enclosed around him. It was apparent that there was an altercation, and the young man in the middle was prepared to give his best fight. This scene took place directly in front of my apartment. I remember hearing little kids' voices and seeing children playing in front of their apartments along this street. I looked to the circle of young men and saw the young man in the middle reach for his pocket, patting it, as though letting the others know that he had a weapon. As he did this, the other young men began visibly preparing themselves. Fear pierced my heart, heart beating quickly, and I kept thinking, "My gosh, there are babies playing out here. What are they doing? Why are they doing this?" I thought of my son sleeping in his car seat as I drove onto the scene. I quickly made a U-turn and drove to the office that was minutes from closing. I jumped out of my car, ran into the rental office, and frantically explained the scene and fear for my son, myself, and the children who lived in nearby apartments. The staff assured me that they were going to call the police as a safety precaution. By this time, I had returned to my car and made the journey to the back of the complex. It had suddenly dawned on me that the young men saw me drive off, so I became frightened that they would retaliate. As I turned down my street, the young men had vanished, and children were seen playing outside. I parked my car and carried my then five-year-old into our apartment. I was stricken with fear. I was afraid that the young men would return once they knew the police had left the premises. It was approximately 6:05 pm. I sat on the dining room floor, encouraging my son to play with his toys and complete his homework. I told my son that we were playing a game of who could stay seated on the floor the longest. The truth was that I was paralyzed with fear that gunshots would ring and pierce through our sliding glass door directly facing the street. The worst thoughts were running through my mind. I did not want my son to know how terrified I was. I did the one thing that I knew would help and that was pray. I laid on that floor for hours until nightfall, praying aloud, praying silently, speaking in my heavenly language, worshipping and praising God for His grace, protection, and wisdom. With tears flowing down my face pleading to God to protect my son and me, I asked God to make way for homeownership in a safe neighborhood. I pleaded for God to make a way, especially when I had been looking to purchase a home for many years prior, going through several realtors, but with a poor credit score and no funds, in the physical realm, it felt impossible. There I was on my knees, with hands lifted to the sky, and my son fast asleep on the dining room floor. I was too afraid to stand up and turn the lights on, so we remained in the dark. Almost five hours later, at 10:30, I prayed for fear to leave me so I could feed my son and get him ready for the next day, which I did. Unbeknownst to me, God would answer that prayer of homeownership one year later.

Why is perseverance and your ability to persevere through challenging moments in your life journey an important topic to address within your co-parenting relationship with Christ and in achieving harmony? Regardless of your age, background, experience, religion, or how you identify spiritually and religiously, we all have and will go through some form of adversity.

At times, people wrongfully assume that because one identifies as a believer of Christ, born-again Christian, we are pardoned from adversity. There is nothing further from the truth. God did not promise us a problem-free, adversity-free, or challenge-free world, but His Word equips us with the ability to move through them, and not only move through the journey, but to do so triumphantly. Yes, you may have received a scar, a bruise, a thorn from the experience, but His Word gives you the strength, the fortitude, the grace, and the wisdom to persevere. Meditate on the following Scripture as you persevere through your troubles.

> *"We are hard pressed on every side, but not crushed; perplexed, but not in despair; persecuted, but not abandoned; struck down, but not destroyed"* (2 Corinthians 4:8-9).

Practical Application

Think back to your most recent trial. Or perhaps it is one you are experiencing currently. Earlier in this chapter, we spoke about reaction versus response. It stems from how one copes with challenges in life. Have you heard of the coping strategies: problem or solution-focused coping and emotion-focused coping? These strategies explain one's mindset on how to cope with a trial that occurs. Problem or solution-focused coping occurs when the individual focuses on how to resolve the stressful problem. This is generally observed as the healthier of the two options because one has learned how to and chooses to respond through critical analysis, age-appropriate judgment, and rationalization. Emotion-focused coping involves moving from a place of emotions, such as not thinking the problem through, not considering all options, long-term effects, and consequences. One *reacts* as opposed to respond. In your journal, discuss this trial in detail, being mindful of feelings that are evoked and the thoughts that flood your mind. Identify the following as it relates to this trial: define what makes this situation challenging, identify previous moments of trials, identify how you moved through the period, identify the strengths that allowed you to move through, and identify the areas that impacted the trial negatively and what you need to improve during this next season. Identify what your God-given purpose is and how this trial plays a role in the grand picture of your God-given purpose. When you have a clear picture of the purpose God has created you for and when you are able to look at the trial from a wider perspective, from a deeper stance, it will guide you on how to maintain spiritual perspective and how to persevere.

Next, explore distractions. Take time to consider and write down areas in your life or people in your life who may be considered distractions that are keeping you from focusing on Jesus during this trial. This may include relationships, whether romantic, friendships, or family. What is the purpose of these relationships? Do these relationships bring you closer to God as you move through this season, or do they distract, hinder, intimidate, or bring anxiety?

Your subsequent step is to identify the emotional and physical symptoms of going through these challenging periods. By identifying these thoughts, feelings, and physical symptoms associated with persevering through trials, you will begin to notice patterns, and ultimately develop a new mindset by implementing a new more healthy pattern as a means to cope when challenges occur.

This practical application section is intended to help you move to a deeper place of self-reflection because believers, especially when not as seasoned, are not informed that because we have chosen to live our lives as born-again Christians, we will not face trials and tribulations. It is vital that we equip ourselves with the tools to move through and persevere when trial seasons make their appearances. To have a clear understanding of the purpose of the trial and understanding how it is defined, what it looks like, and view of the trial from all angles, including physical and emotional signs of perseverance, will strengthen your ability and allow you to get to place of vulnerability to standfast and persevere through.

Applicable Scriptures

"Rejoice always, pray without ceasing, give thanks in all circumstances; for this is the will of God in Christ Jesus for you" (1 Thessalonians 5:17).

"Do not be anxious about anything, but in every situation, by prayer and petition, with thanksgiving, present your requests to God. And the peace of God, which transcends all understanding, will guard your hearts and your minds in Christ Jesus" (Philippians 4:6-7).

"Even though I walk through the darkest valley, I will fear no evil, for you are with me; your rod and your staff, they comfort me" (Psalm 23:4).

"All scripture is breathed out by God and profitable for teaching, for reproof, for correction, and for training in righteousness" (2 Timothy 3:16).

"For whatever was written in former days was written for our instruction, that through endurance and through the encouragement of the Scriptures we might have hope" (Romans 15:4).

"And he told them a parable to the effect that they ought always to pray and not lose heart. He said, "In a certain city there was a judge who neither feared God nor respected man. And there was a widow in that city who kept coming to him and saying, 'Give me justice against my adversary.' For a while he refused, but afterward he said to himself, 'Though I neither fear

God nor respect man yet because this widow keeps bothering me, I will give her justice, so that she will not beat me down by her continual coming'" (Luke 18:1-8).

"And I tell you, ask, and it will be given to you; seek, and you will find; knock, and it will be opened to you. For everyone who asks receives, and the one who seeks finds, and to the one who knocks it will be opened" (Luke 11:9-10).

"As for you, brothers, do not grow weary in doing good" (2 Thessalonians 3:13).

"And let us not grow weary of doing good, for in due season we will reap, if we do not give up" (Galatians 6:9).

"I press on toward the goal for the for the prize of the upward call of God in Christ Jesus" (Philippians 3:14).

"Therefore, my beloved brothers, be steadfast, immovable, always abounding in the work of the Lord, knowing that in the Lord your labor is not in vain" (1 Corinthians 15:58).

"Since we are surrounded by so great a cloud of witnesses, let us also lay aside every weight, and sin which clings so closely, and let us run with endurance the race that is set before us, looking to Jesus, the founder and perfecter of our faith, who for the joy that was set before him endured the cross, despising the shame, and is seated at the right hand of the throne of God" (Hebrews 12:1-2).

Prayer

Heavenly Father, I thank You for all seasons, including the trials and tribulations, for they help to shape me, mold me, and develop me and my character into the woman You have called me to become. Help me and guide me to change my perspective, to essentially have a paradigm shift in how I perceive challenges in my life and my ability to persevere through those challenges. Father, guide me with the tools to discern the physical and emotional symptoms of enduring trials and the ability to stay focused on God. During my times of trials, may my circle of influence be mighty vessels of Your light and glory meant to encourage, empower, and uplift. Heavenly Father, bless me with the gift of discernment so I may have the ability to recognize distractions, may it be something or someone, I ask God to purge all negativity out of my life. Give me Your strength to persevere through the challenges of life. For I know that life as a believer does not keep me from experiencing trials, but Your grace and Your Word equip me with the ability to persevere through it.

Part I Review

BEFORE WE MOVE INTO CHAPTER FOUR, LET us review what we have discussed thus far in the last three chapters of Part I, and how it prepares us as we move forward in this book. We spoke on the importance of understanding the difference between who you are in Christ and the roles that we play in our life. In this regard, we delved into how prayer, journaling, and fasting can be vital tools in strengthening our relationship with Christ and ultimately develop our character and identity in Christ. Next, we jumped into understanding our God-designed and God-given purpose and how knowing this God truth can prepare us in identifying God's mission and vision in our lives. One important piece in developing the character of God in creating a solid foundation in Christ, identity-strengthening, and purpose-finding is understanding how to recognize trials. And understanding how to persevere through them triumphantly. We concluded the chapter by discussing Scriptures that offer guidance on endurance and persevering through the trials of life as you move through your parenting journey while tending to your well-being.

Part Two

As for Me and My House, We Will Serve the Lord

PART 1 IS AN INTEGRAL PIECE TO THE CO-PARenting journey with Christ. The ability to establish your identity in God and differentiate between the various roles you may play and who you have been called to be are key concepts to grasp before moving forward. As women, we are called and often socialized to be nurturers, the heart of the home, and the person of substantial influence in the lives of those we touch daily. This is an amazing responsibility, yet can be a daunting reality for some. We live in a world where we are asked to be many things for many people as each situation provides opportunity to wear a different hat and enter a new realm that we must successfully navigate through. It is difficult to accomplish the tasks of the many roles we play if we do not know who we are, who has called us, and the purpose He has destined us to live out and walk in. As you begin to delve into the mighty Book of God, seek His heart through prayer, journaling, worship, and fasting. Through a receptive heart, He begins to reveal your purpose, vision, and mission in His unique timing and in His way. While understanding and learning how to walk in your purpose, you will encounter challenges in life that require endurance. Once you are able to achieve the foundational concepts, it opens opportunity for the next step: laying the foundation for your home and your family.

In this section, *As for me and my house, we will serve the Lord,* I cover chapters four through six, which focus on the heart of the family, the function of the family, parenting and your relationship with your children, and your identity within the home. We then change gears by becoming in tune with your role as a mother, and the various lens in which we see and navigate through life that impacts how we experience our world in chapters six and seven. We conclude Part II with a thorough look at dating and courtship as a beautiful, classy and sassy, God-fearing woman in chapter eight.

Chapter 4

Home is Where the Heart Is

"For no one can lay a foundation other than that which is laid, which is Jesus Christ" (1 Corinthians 3:11).

WE OFTENTIMES HEAR THE PHRASE, *HOME IS where the heart is*, but have you asked yourself what it truly means? Or perhaps what this statement means for you, your household, and your family? Up to this point in our journey, we have discussed identity and roles, purpose, calling, and vision. Likewise, we have explored how you recognize, develop, and strengthen your ability to persevere. Now it is time to delve into your home, your children, and your relationship with your children. Foundation within the home is a vital piece to the puzzle. Foundation and the well-being of your sacred place and haven from the outside world is the next step to achieving harmony in your single-parent journey. When you think of *foundation*, what does that look like in your eyes? As it relates to your family, what are the necessary items that create your home's foundation? Is it faith? Is it sound teaching? Is it parenting style? Is it health or emotional well-being? Does a sense of togetherness create foundation for your home? Does it involve structure or perhaps a more flexible and informal approach? Describe what that picture entails in your world and apply it as you read further.

For me and my household, my foundation shifted as my faith deepened and strengthened.

When I gave my life wholeheartedly to Christ, He began to reveal areas in my life that He wanted to heal, restore, mold, shape, rebuild, and this included my home life. I can recall the moment when it became clear that foundation was meant to be the center of life. For instance, when I first stepped into a supervisorial role, I asked my manager what she and the department's expectations were of me as a supervisor. She responded, "Good question! I expect you to read, review, research, study, analyze, provide substantial feedback, and know what you're talking about, and if you don't know, then know where to go find the information to make a sound decision." She elaborated, "How can I expect you to train, support, and educate your staff if you don't know yourself?" So similar to my home life as the leader in my home as a single parent-headed household, how could I expect positive results and how could I expect to lead my family of two and establish a legacy of godliness without having an understanding and wisdom on the One whom a foundation was predicated upon. When I became a born-again believer, I soaked in the Word and sought to dwell in the Holy Spirit, constantly reading, studying, and analyzing. God began showing me how to apply what I was learning in His Word to my everyday life. The Word is my foundation. It is what gives me life. It is what gives me breath. It is what gives me understanding, hope for the future, correction when I have made mistakes, guidance and direction when I am at a loss, peace and solace in chaos, joy, and not just happiness, but pure joy and strength and perseverance in my most challenging seasons.

His Word says, "In the beginning was the Word, and the Word was with God, and the Word was God" (John 1:1). So let me ask you dear one, where does your foundation lie?

Over the years, I had become involved in various ministries, including women's ministry, convalescent center, homeless and community outreach, and facilitating single mothers' ministry, all while working full time, pursuing my doctorate, maintaining a home, being involved in the community and my son's school committees, and raising a God-fearing child. And somewhere in the midst of this, I was trying to have an active dating and social life. Yet, I could not understand why I was so physically exhausted and why my home felt unstructured as though it was barely holding on by a thread.

In late 2017, life began to unravel as I frequently fell ill, making ungodly choices, and feeling overwhelmed. I attempted to hold on to the various ministries that I was involved in. I attempted to continue my participation in the many community, social, and personal obligations until my home life had enough. For years, I had attempted to "multi-task," until I was told that there was no such thing as multitasking because it is impossible to tend to various tasks with the same level of time, commitment, and energy. And what results is spreading oneself too thin. As I felt like the world was closing in around me, I sought God for guidance and understanding. It was my way of control or feeling as though I had control over every aspect of my life. Areas in my life needed finetuning, revision, remediation, and elimination. As I was preparing for a lesson for an upcoming single mother ministry meeting, I recall God whispering in my spirit, "How was I to give what I didn't have? How was I to teach what I did not understand? How was I to help them implement strategies that I had not yet learned or even knew was an issue for me?" "Wow!" I thought. I immediately repented and invited God on this journey to remove things and situations out of my life. God began to show me by saying, "Home is your first ministry." Have you ever seen individuals involved in two, three, five or more ministries at the church where they are in a position of leadership, yet their house, their marriage, their children have gone astray, or problems abound in their home? Yes, things happen, and yes, sometimes out of our control, despite our fight and resolve. However, when we begin to see patterns of continuous dysfunction and do not address it, and when we displace the energy and time that we should be placing in our homes onto areas outside of the home, then there is need for concern. God began showing me that if I did not address the lack of spiritual foundation in my home at that moment, it would manifest in a more serious consequence in the future.

The Scripture, "Draw near to God and He will draw near to you" (James 4:8) comes to mind as I sought divine guidance. So as I began to draw nearer to my Heavenly Father, He drew nearer to me in His presence, in His Word, and through revelation, guiding me for my home and family. I fasted, journaled, and sought spiritual wisdom. To this day, whenever I am heading towards the opposite direction in my parenting choices, I experience night dreams involving my relationship with my son. For me, this serves as a warning to lead with wisdom and change my path.

God revealed that it was time to respond as God called me to, and the doors began to close. Obligations began to shift. Everything must be done in decency and in order. As community and social obligations dwindled and others stepped in to take on these responsibilities and positions of authority, structure began to fill my home and our lives. God would speak to me through journaling in areas where we were strong as a family. God would show me areas that required improvement, such as strategies on how to implement routines, creating intentional quality time, and no social phone calls Sunday through Thursday night, learning effective communication skills, and asking for help from people within our circle (grandparents, close friends, son's school staff). And most importantly, I developed both structured and unstructured time for frequent self-check in and family assessments. A paradigm shift began to occur as God began taking every realm in my life, piece by piece, to examine it and put it back into place renewed, whole, and restored.

Home Is Your First Ministry

"Through wisdom, a house is built, and by understanding it is established; by knowledge the rooms are filled with all precious and pleasant riches" (Proverbs 24:3-4).

When you think of ministry, you may naturally and spiritually equate the term to that of, pertaining to, or involving the church (building) and serving the Church (body of Christ), but when exploring the term ministry, we must explore how this term relates to our family as well. Ministry involves giving of oneself, a level of self-sacrifice, being of service, and being an expression of God and love to others. Watering our family, essentially providing our family with the tools to flourish, is a part of ministry.

As women, we may have a tendency to be a part of and involved in several organizations, situations, and ministries, whether that is in the traditional or non-traditional sense of the word ministry. Perhaps it is focusing on volunteering in a ministry daily after work until eight in the evening, all day Saturday, and before and after church on Sundays, while the individual's marriage is not being tended to, or the home life and structure is in shambles. This is not a moment of being judgmental and critical of others, but what I am hoping that you will gain from this conversation is to pay attention to themes that you observe in your life, and where we can improve because there is *always* room for improvement. Be mindful that different seasons, events, and various contributing factors may change one's dynamics at any given time. However, for a short time frame and with communication with your significant other, if present, and family, it may prove to be appropriate. But if this short season becomes a long-term lifestyle, then it is time to acknowledge the current state, what changes need to occur, and how and when to implement the new strategies so you and your family may live the life that God has called you to live.

God is a God of decency and of order as is shared in 1 Corinthians 14:33, "For God is not a God (not the author) of disorder (confusion), but of peace. As in all the churches of the saints." With that said, our home and our family is our first ministry. After God and your relationship with Him, who follows next? I have heard many women say that their children come before their husbands or their parents come before their spouses, or even the church affairs and ministry takes precedence over their place of employment. This is not the correct order. Take for instance, "He must be one who manages his own household well, keeping his children under control with all dignity (but if a man does not know how to manage his own household, how will he take care of the church of God), and not a new convert, so that he will not become conceited and fall into the condemnation incurred by the devil" (1 Timothy 3:4). God is the head, followed by your spouse (when married), your children, your employment, and ministry and other affairs and obligations. You may ask, where do you fit into this hierarchy? Maintaining your emotional well-being and overall self-care is imperative and ranks high in this chart of priority. We will delve more into self-care and emotional well-being in a later chapter, but know that caring for others and being wife, mother, ministry leader, employee, and volunteer should not involve constant self-sacrifice at the expense of your sanity, your health, and your self-care. Let us begin to unravel and apply this knowledge to one area at a time in your life.

Structure

"He is before all things, and in Him all things hold together" (Colossians 1:17).

Written from a single-mother perspective, I share my experiences from the perspective of a woman raising her children without other adults in the home. However, it is imperative to express the importance of having a spiritual male father figure, godfather, or male role model who, those of you who are single, raising or not raising children, may go to for sound wisdom, guidance, and advice. In my case, as a single woman, my father (biological) is my spiritual head, who covers me and my household.

As we delve into the importance of structure, it is vital to first define it. According to Merriam-Webster Dictionary (2020), *structure* is defined as, "construct or arrange according to a plan; give a pattern or organization to." Another definition explains structure as "the arrangement of and relations between the parts or elements of something complex." One God-given strategy that proved to be essential in my co-parenting relationship with Christ was structure within the home. Essentially, I view structure as the vision that I see for my home and family. Where did I see my family one year from now, three years, five years, even ten or twenty years from now when my grandchildren are in the picture as I foresee the legacy that God has called me to leave behind? Every layer in my life was peeled back to expose the core and the foundation from which my home had to be based on. This occurred both figuratively and in the most practical terms. As I had mentioned, the first step in being true to home being my first ministry was understanding my identity in Christ, how that impacted my home and interaction with my son, and my purpose and calling. The next step was allowing God to close doors of the various ministries, activities, and social events I was involved in. There was a time when I had to be at every conference, event, baby shower, wedding, birthday celebration, meeting, hike, or social gathering. I was involved in every school committee and frequently volunteered my son for any and all mentorship programs and extracurricular activities on top of an already hectic lifestyle. This continued for years until I found myself exhausted, priorities had shifted with the most essential tasks being pushed to the very bottom, and my son's grades were suffering. Through journaling, fasting, and prayer, God revealed that I was overcompensating for "the lack."

What is meant by "the lack?" The lack of a spouse, the lack of a partner, the lack of time, lack of energy, lack of funds, lack of the elaborate lifestyle and lavish house, lack of having everything together at any given moment, and ultimately, the lack of control or what I thought was control. It was a facade that was harming myself and my family. The "lack" mentality needed to be healed and restored to the mentality of "complete" and "wholeness." We live in a society that refers to single-mother-headed households as "broken" and single women as incomplete, lacking, incapable, or even inferior to our married counterparts. I remember being 30 years old, having purchased my home one year before, completed my masters' degree, and while visiting family, a family friend said, "You better hurry up and find someone. You're getting up there. You need to hurry up, find somebody, so you can have more kids." Now, in hindsight, there are so many concerns that come to mind with this mindset of hers, but at the time, I was completely oblivious to what was being said to me. I knew that thirty was still quite young, as statistically speaking, more adults were waiting well into their thirties and even forties to get married and have children after they have pursued their education and climbed up the career ladder. This was especially the case for women. When it began to sink in with what she was implying, my response was that I was doing pretty good. I had time for that next season, and I had no regrets with where I was in my life in that season. When I was completing my doctoral dissertation, article after article, text after text, these were the adjectives that described unmarried and unpartnered single mothers- again, terms such as broken, impoverished, and ghetto. Some suggested that I use these terms to describe the single-mother experience, and I fought adamantly against it. But understand that this was a paradigm shift that needed to take place within as the foundation of my family was being rebuilt. This now leads me to leadership style and the strategies you apply in leading your home.

Leadership Style

"When a country is rebellious, it has many rulers, but a ruler with discernment and knowledge maintains order" (Proverbs 28:2).

Leadership style, you may ask, what does that have to do with creating structure in the home and providing a foundation in the home? In short, everything. You may hear some well-known theorists refer to the home as being run as a business with the parent(s) being the leader and employer, where everyone has a role and the parent makes all final decisions. There are others who believe in the importance of incorporating the children's views and opinions into all decision-making. And then there are those who fall somewhere within this spectrum. Where do you stand? Assess how you lead your family because whether you are aware of it or not, proactive about your approach or not, you are leading and guiding your family, and that may be good, bad, or indifferent. Some leadership styles that you may hear in the workplace, church, or place, where one or more are placed in a position of authority, include transactional leadership, transformational leadership, democratic or participative approach, directive approach, delegation, and collaboration to name a few. The one similarity that lies between leadership styles and parenting styles is that no one employs the same style. Why? Because you are working with individuals of various personalities and not every leadership style may be applied for every person and with every situation presented. An individual in a leadership position may favor one over the other or frequently lean towards one or two styles. The leadership and parenting style you employ will oftentimes be situational, meaning that your style may be tailored by the situation as it occurs. As we discussed leadership style, we will explore parenting.

Parenting

"Children are a heritage of the Lord, and the fruit of the womb is a reward" (Psalm 127:3).

"Train up a child in the way he should go and when he is old, he will not depart" (Proverbs 22:6).

The aforementioned Scriptures are two of my favorite verses that speak to parenting. Parenting, your relationship with your children, and your ability to lead your family are all monumental. We, as women of God, must have positive and godly influence as we speak into the lives of others. Let us first define parenting. According to Bristow, Faircloth, Lee, and Macvarish (2014), a distinction between child-rearing and parenting exists with child-rearing, essentially being applied more in a historical context towards agricultural societies where children were expected to participate in the work and routine of the community. In more current times, child-rearing is a term to describe the parent's role as the provider of shelter, clothing, and food. The authors emphasized that this term child-rearing evolved into the term parenting. As parents, we are expected to provide special parenting attention and understand that parents' actions impact the child's development in addition to the provisional parental obligations as observed in child-rearing. Parenting involves more than physical care, but psychological care, emotional and overall well-being of children, their future, and the legacy they leave on this world as adults when we as their mothers have gone on to be with God.

In the world of research, one term that is frequently applied within parenting is intensive mothering. Intensive mothering is frequently used to refer to the ideal mother, one who is foremost a caregiver and invests almost unattainable amounts of time, money, energy, and emotional labor into raising her children to the point of continuously potentially sacrificing her own emotional and physical well-being. Intensive mothering, or also known as "good mothering," has cultural implications, and people from different levels of socioeconomic status and ethnic background may experience this concept differently. Intensive mothering involves more than the "normal duties" or function of mothering, and mothers of color are reported to require to take into account how race relations may affect their children and additional considerations not experienced by all mothers. To elaborate, women of color, in particular women of the African American and Latino community who are mothers of adolescents, report a substantially larger rate than their Caucasian counterparts to engage in activities and behaviors that "protect" their children. The authors refer to the term *protect* as activities and behaviors, especially within impoverished and metropolitan areas, that occur when mothers ensure that their adolescent males are not participating in crime, violence, gang membership, or other deviant behavior. Additionally, concerns with encounters with law enforcement and authority figures in recent years have been reported at significantly higher rates and are covered under intensive mothering for the single mother of color.

Here are some questions to ponder: How do you view parenting? What constitutes being a good mother in your eyes? How did you come to this conclusion? Did your parent or guardian's parenting style impact your current parenting views? How did your mother or mother-figure interact with you and the family? Were your parents in your life? Do you see being a mother as a role that you play or part of your identity? Does the culture and how you were raised, or people you surround yourself with now, impact your mothering? Are there additional factors that you take into consideration as a mother? Think about these questions as you assess your upbringing, your parenting style, areas you would like to improve in your parenting, and strategies on how to improve. It is difficult to have a discussion about parenting without exploring the various parenting styles that we employ in our homes.

Parenting Styles

What does your relationship look like with your children? Do your children feel comfortable sharing the day's events with you? Can they trust you with their heart? Are you their safe haven? Do they respond to you out of fear?

Have you heard of the terms *authoritative, authoritarian, permissive*, and *neglectful*? These terms are traditionally known as the four parenting styles coined by Dr. Diana Baumrind (1967). The premise of the parenting styles was that the development of the child and the interaction with their parents, and more specifically, the actions of the parent towards the child impact the child behaviorally, emotionally, and cognitively. Baumrind (1967) emphasized the frequency and intensity of demandingness (parents' expectations based on results and productivity) and warmth and acceptance (parents' sensitivity to children's emotional needs). As we move forward, take note of which styles resonate with you.

Authoritative style is regarded as being high in both demand-ingness and warmth and acceptance. This looks like parents having the ability to balance between being emotionally in-tune to their children's emotional needs and providing a structured environment with a consistent set of rules. Parents of this style help children to develop problem-solving and analytical skills. Children tend to be more creative, resourceful, sociable, and independent thinkers. How would this translate in the practical sense, you may ask? This may involve such activities as super-vising their children's academic performance, setting curfews, implementing chores, providing incentives and reward systems, and structured healthy discipline. Parents tend to be emotion-ally engaged, such as noticing when their child's behavior, atti-tude, or mood changes, having consistent check-ins with the child to gauge the child's emotions and thought process.

Children raised with an authoritative parenting environment are reported to have higher academic grades, higher self-esteem, more healthy social skillset, can easily adapt to challenging situ-ations, and are less reported to be diagnosed with certain mood and anxiety disorders.

Research suggests that the authoritative parenting style is the most healthy and ideal environment to raise children. On the opposite end of the spectrum lies the neglectful parenting style, which is a parent who provides an environment with little to no emotional support. It may also include lack of physical attachment with little effort. In this type of parenting, or lack thereof, the parent is described and experienced by the child as cold, emotionally detached, unresponsive, and uninvolved. Children raised in this type of environment are reported to be more susceptible to experiencing and being diagnosed with mental illness, experience addictions and engaging in addictive behaviors, and engaging in deviant behavior as teens and adults. This type of environment may look like a home in which the parent is not engaged in the child's overall well-being psychologically, financially, cognitively, or physically. There are various factors that may contribute to this type of interaction, such as the upbringing of the parent and untreated, undiagnosed, or poorly managed mental illness, not having the proper supports in place, and uneducated of where to go to access those resources, or overall, not having an environment that is conducive for children.

Signs that a child is living in a neglectful environment may include a combination of behaviors. For instance, school personnel may notice a student who arrives daily appearing disheveled or unkempt, with poor attendance, perhaps does not appear to have food to eat for breakfast, or may be engaging in deviant behavior, such as smoking, drinking alcohol, gang activity, drugs, self-harm, attempting to harm others including siblings, and criminal activity. These are red flags that cause concern. Do note that the presence of these behaviors or observations may not determine neglectful behavior on the caregivers, but should be monitored. For those of us who are mandated reporters in the helping profession, should you have any concerns, please report via telephone and in written form to your state or county governmental agency who investigates abuse towards minors. Remember that if you are not an employee of these agencies, you may report any suspected abuse, but it is not your duty to investigate the abuse as your state has designated certified individuals to do so.

Permissive parenting involves parents who express high affection, warmth, and acceptance towards their children. The permissive parent does not provide a structured environment. This means a home environment that lacks in consistent set of rules and appropriate discipline. Gaille (2017) suggests that children being raised in this type of environment exhibit impulsive behavior, lack discipline or limited self-control, and are more susceptible to being diagnosed with a personality disorder. Parents of this mindset may be heard saying, "I'm my child's friend. We do X, Y, Z together."

Baumrind's (1967) fourth style, the authoritarian parenting style, emphasizes structure, discipline, consistent set of rules with focus on results, and productivity. An authoritarian parent does not express affection, warmth, or acceptance. This type of parenting leaves little opportunity for the child to develop independence, critical thinking, or analytical skills. According to Eyberg, Querido, and Warner (2002) suggested that previous research indicated that the authoritarian style is most often observed by mothers of color, especially African American women. However, Eyberg, Querido, and Warner (2002) reexamined the notion whether racial interactions contributes to this specific parenting style indicating that a correlation may not exist. Oftentimes, parents of this style are considered "too strict." Children raised in this parenting environment are reported to have lower academic grades and self-esteem and are observed as having poor social skills with low ability to healthfully cope with emotionally difficult situations.

In more recent years, another form of parenting styles was introduced into the world of research. According to Leifer and Fleck (2013), some parents implement one of three more current parenting styles: autocratic, democratic, or laissez-faire style. Someone implementing an autocratic style is someone who makes decisions without any input from the children in the family. Children who are raised in a laissez-faire environment experience an abundance of freedom where parents provide "complete freedom for all members, with no rules, minimal discipline (if any), and no effort at impulse control (Leifer and Fleck 2013, 48)." And the final parenting style, the democratic style, was one in which there is healthy communication, and both the parent and the child(ren) participate in decision-making. In the democratic parenting style, a mutual level of respect exists between the parent and the child(ren). The hope is that as a parent, allow God to equip you as a parent to prevent dysfunction. As a functional family, your role as a parent is to develop a stable unit, a family environment in which rules are established, members are healthfully equipped to cope with stress and conflict, and foster overall well-being.

Parenting styles and the actions that parents elicit toward their children is a vital part of a child's upbringing. If you have not already, reflect on the parenting style of your childhood and the style that was most prevalent. The parenting style that you may veer towards as adults may be influenced by the parents' cultural backgrounds (Leifer and Fleck, 2013, 48). Have you heard of the term *differentiation*? It is a term we apply in psychology that derived from Bowen's family theory. Differentiation is having the ability to separate from your own emotions from the emotions of other people (self-differentiation) and separate your experience from the experience of others (interpersonal differentiation). Both levels of differentiation involves a level of self-awareness. What makes this concept applicable to parenting is the fact that differentiation explores the reality that children's behavior, symptoms, and the like are a "byproduct of, and interrelated with the dynamics and structure of their family (Takieddine 2017)." Furthermore, we are not immune to emotions of people around us. Contrary to that fact, our emotions and sense of who we are, are influenced by the emotional system, or lack thereof, that is created in the family.

How did your parents emotionally address difficult situations? As challenges arose, did your parent or parents respond or react? What am I asking you? Did your parent or parents react from an emotionally unstable place wrapped in anger with yelling, crying, or even with a physical streak, possibly with a manipulative tone, for instance? Did they address situations from an emotionally healthy place with the ability to cope with and move through the difficulty? Yes, we all may have a tendency to become emotionally unsound at times, but it is what you do with those emotions and how you move forward through the situation that I want you to focus on. Do you allow yourself to become controlled by the emotion? How did your parents' emotional response or reaction influence you and how you interact with your children today? Did your parents seem aloof and unattached? Perhaps they were warm, gentle, and compassionate. Were you raised with having a set of consistent rules, chores, and sound discipline? How do you address situations now as an adult? How do you manage your emotions or do they control you now as an adult? Do you see a correlation between your emotional upbringing and parenting style of your parents and the emotional upbringing of your children and the parenting style that you elicit with your children? We will delve more into this during the practical application of this chapter. But for now, allow us to continue with a discussion on the home environment while keeping these questions in mind.

Providing a Sound and Faith-Based Environment

What does your home environment look like? Is it welcoming? Is it stuffy or airy, with air freely flowing throughout the home?

I am reminded of my dear sister in Christ, Elizabeth, who has since gone to be with the Lord. Elizabeth and I worked together, and she played an integral role in me, not only giving my life to Christ, but deepening my faith and strengthening my relationship with God. As time went on, Elizabeth would invite my son and I to join her and her family at their home for Bible studies and fellowship. Sometimes this would occur with only she and I or an intimate group of lady friends. And other times, she and her family would hold Saturday night studies with twenty or more people that included praise and worship, food, Bible study, prayer, praise reports, and fellowship, and at times, preparing gifts and shipments to send to other countries. Everyone enjoyed going to Elizabeth and her family's home. I absolutely cherished those times and hold them dear to my heart. It was a different feeling once I entered her home every single time. Once I walked into the home, the peace and joy that would fall upon me was indescribable. It was as though, even if I had not known Elizabeth, I would know that their home was a home of prayer. It was a place where the Holy Spirit dwelled in every room of their home from the very moment I stepped onto the property. Elizabeth would, at times, have candles, praise and worship music, and always had food and healthy choices that contributed to this feeling of warmth and welcome. She was careful in decorating to the detail during the Christmas season and was frequently shedding her closet and storage to give items away, whether to friends (including me), family, or strangers. As I would observe the interactions between Elizabeth and her family, their relationship was pure, loving, and always cherished and tended to in love and with love. And that was how Elizabeth was toward her friends and everyone who knew her. It was a home where contrite and strife were not felt, but a home you knew God took the authority in the home. It was not "just a house," but a home. I remember telling myself, yes, this is what peace felt like.

As the woman of the home, you set the stage for how you want others to feel in your home. Is your house just a house? What do I mean by that? Have you been living in your space for five years and still have boxes that you have yet to unpack? Does your house appear as though you are only visiting, or have you taken ownership of what God has blessed you with? Transition from making your "house" into a "home." Physically, do not be afraid to decorate (depending on the age of your children), light candles, or consider bringing fresh flowers in the home or spray a lovely fragrance throughout the home, thoroughly clean your home, and enlist your kids in this endeavor. Perhaps what makes a house into a home for you is cooking a beautiful meal for your loved ones. Maybe it is the aroma-filled Sunday family dinners. You may feel that a family pet adds a sense of homeliness. Or you may feel having frequent social gatherings or your friends and your children's friends and family over occasionally makes your house feel like a home. Explore what a sense of home, physically and spiritually, means for you and your family.

Now, allow us to discuss how to implement faith and spirituality into your everyday life. What does this look like? Allow me to share a story with you. Yes, I am full of stories! I began my house-hunting journey in 2005, shortly after I moved my then three-year-old son and myself into an apartment. I worked with various realtors. My son and I would go on mini adventures to look at potential houses. By the summer of 2010, so much had occurred within my personal life, and I was believing God for a change. I had looked at eighteen properties, had put in an offer three to five times in five years, and with poor credit, the hope was barely glimmering. A spiritual mentor, an older single mother, whom I had befriended through work, met a gentleman who worked for a lending company. She had great success as he helped her purchase an investment property. So I began working with him, and he introduced me to a realtor who was equally amazing. My prayer wish list was not long. I prayed for the right home that was the right fit, did not have to be fancy, required minimal repairs if needed, and in a safe and family-oriented neighborhood with great schools.

The realtor and I had looked at several properties, and on this last one, she was not able to make it, so she sent me to the property. And on this Saturday morning, my son and I walked into this one-story house that was located exactly one neighborhood over from my parents' home. I knew this was it. It felt right. I instantly called the realtor while standing in the house and said, "This is it. I just know it It feels like our home. I want to put in an offer." She responded, "Absolutely, let's do it. I'll draft it up. Now get out of the house, so people don't discover that you aren't a realtor." I complied, but before I did, God reminded me of the anointing oil that I had in a tiny bottle in my purse. God whispered in my spirit to anoint and pray over the house. Suddenly, I realized God's strategic plan to "prevent" my realtor from joining my son and me on this house tour. There I was, trying not to bring attention to myself with the neighbors outside. I began declaring and decreeing that, "Father if it be Your will," placing a dot of anointing oil over every door and every window, binding any ungodliness from owners before me, praying aloud, praying in my heavenly language, and claiming this house as our home. My then seven-year-old followed behind, and by that point, he was accustomed to Mom's loud praying. This was in early August 2010, and I had been on a month-to-month pricey lease with my apartment, believing by faith that I would not need to sign another six-month lease with my apartment manager. The offer was made, and at the last moment, I was told to make the final call to my retirement plan that Monday to withdraw the funds to make the down payment on my home. I called, nonchalantly expecting a "Yes, Ms. Serano, we'll get that money to you within the next seven to ten business days." What I heard on the other end of that call was, "I'm sorry, Ms. Serano, that is only available for those who allocated an additional employee contribution, and you did not do this." I sat there on the bedroom floor, listening to my son playing in his room, and I was disheartened. Tears could no longer flow because there were not any left. I started to ask, "Why and how is it not my time, Lord, because I've been faithful. I'm trying to be faithful. I did not know what else to do, so I began dialing the number of random friends who knew my heart's desire. No one picked up. I called my lender with worry in my voice and told him that it was over. He said, "No, it's not. Continue to believe, Chanel. This is going to work out. Make some calls. This is going to work out!" This is why this gentleman, who is a believer and follower of Jesus Christ, is my friend to this day because he allowed God to use him as a vessel to speak life into me and into a situation that I thought was dead.

A few days after, I began to feel that homeownership was not meant for me. Doubt began to find its way into my mind. My dear friend, who I spoke of earlier, called me and said, "My daughter and I have money in the bank. I spoke with my daughter, and after prayer, we feel led to loan you some money to put towards a down payment." I was in disbelief, with tears flowing. The down payment amount was not the total amount required, but when you do not have any additional funds, any amount over one hundred dollars is like thousands of dollars. I thanked her and requested some time to pray about the remaining down payment. Within days, a friend who I had met some time before offered to loan me the remaining amount. Within one week, this obstacle was resolved, and both of whom I paid back within one year. And on September 30, 2010, my son and I moved into our home.

What did this experience teach me about leadership and handling challenges? Over the years of being in our home, from day one of first seeing our home, I strived to instill a sound and faith-based environment. Did I always succeed? No. Did I get it right every time or most of the time? Quite sure, I did not. Did I make mistakes along the way and failed to do things God's way in God's timing? Oh, absolutely. But His grace is sufficient. God is the leader of our home and our family.

God revealed several tools that strengthened our relationship with Christ, strengthened my parenting relationship with my son, and provided a structured faith-based environment. These tools included family Bible studies, daily discussions and quality time with my son, and financial and life lessons to my son. What tools are you equipping your family with? What processes have you implemented in your home? Now let us move on into another way that you can ensure that your home is your first ministry: incorporating family Bible time.

Family Bible Time

I continue to grow in this area and strive to make our family Bible study time a priority, weekly. This time is separate from attending church or being involved in ministry. It is a time when my son and I devote time to not only read the Word, but study and apply it to everyday life. For my home, my son and I try to allocate family Bible study once, weekly, typically on a Sunday or a day or timeframe when we will have uninterrupted time. We spend the first twenty to thirty minutes having private individual time with God when we each read and study a Bible chapter and or teen devotion for my son. After we have studied the Bible and spoken to God, my son and I will meet up and open our family Bible study session with prayer. Prayer for asking God to bring clarity, wisdom, and understanding to the text, prayer to forgive us of any sins that we have individually committed, prayer to be in a place of surrender, and be receptive to what God has to teach us. This opening prayer is followed by a discussion of what we have read. We have three rules for our individual and family Bible study: 1) provide a synopsis or summary of what was read, 2) what was learned or understood from the text, and 3) how we may apply the selected text to our everyday life by giving both real-life and hypothetical examples. For instance, my son may share an experience that he had at school with his friends and would discuss how he addressed the concern, what and how he would improve his response, and share his strengths in that situation. I, too, follow the same rules as I share the details of my reading with my son.

Our synopsis of our individual Bible study time is followed by reading a chapter in the Bible. We do not have a particular "formula" in which book of the Bible we focus on unless God leads me to a specific book, chapter, or Scripture. My son and I take turns reading the selected chapter and discuss. This time, focusing on God's Word provides an opportunity for quality time while building our relationship with Christ. Family Bible studies hone in on the importance of not only reading the Bible, but studying the Bible, and more importantly, having the ability to apply the Word in every aspect of our lives. The Word becomes alive in our lives. Incorporating individual and family Bible study time has been monumental in providing a sound faith-based environment.

What is your family regimen when it comes to reading the Bible? Is reading the Bible of importance? For those who enjoy studying the Bible, I am hopeful that you understand the impact that it has on your life. It is life-changing. I am not one to remember every Scripture or every chapter of every book of the Bible, but in my most challenging, fearful, and uncertain times, Scriptures will suddenly pop up in my spirit. If you and your family have a current Bible study structure, evaluate how this designated time is working with you and your family? Do you have a planned day of the week, planned time of day, or timeframe? Is there need for improvement? Keep in mind that if you do not have any regimen in place, consider how you are able to not only incorporate this time, but make family Bible time a priority. And know that you and your family should make this time tailored to the needs of your family and not compared to other families. This quality time with God and with your family will improve, strengthen, and nourish your relationship with your children.

Relationship with Our Children

"And these words that I command you today shall be on your heart. You shall teach them diligently to your children, and shall talk of them when you sit in your house, and when you walk by the way, and when you lie down, and when you rise. You shall bind them as a sign on your hand, and they shall be as frontlets between your eyes. You shall write them on the doorposts of your house and on your gates" (Deuteronomy 6:6-9).

Now that we have discussed the leadership style as the leader of your home and the parenting style of you, as a mother, let us delve into your relationship with your children. Go ahead. I will wait. The interaction that you share with your children is more than an encounter, it is a relationship. Whether you are aware of this truth or not, how you connect with your children, how you speak with your children, how your children feel safe and protected is impacted by your relationship with them. I have observed many relationships between parents and their children over the years, with some appearing healthy, some eliciting a high level of dysfunction, and others constantly evolving and shifting. One relationship stuck with me. In theory and from the outside, this family appeared strong and healthy with what the world considered as perfect. The family was a two-parent household, living in a house they purchased in a middle-class neighborhood; the children attended a great school, the father working a well-paying job, and the mother having the choice to not work outside of the home. The father was raised in a home where the father worked outside of the home, and his mother stayed at home, caring for the children. When he grew up, married, and had a family of his own, the couple decided to raise their family in a similar fashion. The father ensured that he provided financially, and was observed to be emotionally removed from the parenting related to what he observed as a child, the mother was observed to be the disciplinarian, emotional and physical caretaker, and ensured that the monies were spent according to budget. As their oldest grew up and had her own children, she began to reflect on her own upbringing, noticing that her relationship with her mother was strained, feeling as though she was raised with fear being the primary motivator. Fear of disappointing her family, fear of developing her own voice, and fear of having an opinion different from her mother plagued her in her early adult years and in early years of being a mother. It had an impact on her relationship with her mother and changed the trajectory of her own relationship with her children, vowing to not raise her children out of fear and to work on developing her own children's voice.

Let us not impair or poorly equip our children for the world by instilling a spirit of fear, but of power, love, and of sound mind as the Bible says. She valued, taught, and expected her children to develop independent, critical-thinking skills while ensuring that they speak their mind, but being respectful in how they did so. Do not quench the spirit, encourage your children to think for themselves and to know that it is acceptable if they do not agree with your stance, especially as they get older. As parents, let us be mindful of the tendency to raise and teach our children out of fear and from a place of fear. For instance, a child may be afraid of coming home past curfew for fear of his or her parent. Some parents may see this as a positive feeling while others may see this as indifferent. It may be a fear of disappointing their parents or fear of being caught for the punishment that follows. I want to pose a question to you. Would you want your child to have a fear of you, a fear of displeasing God, or both? I would hope that children do not intentionally want to disappoint their parents, but the ultimate hope for all of us as parents should be that our children have a higher desire to please God because in pleasing God, they will ultimately honor us as their parents. How do we teach that motivation in our children? How do we teach our legacy lived through our children to have the internal desire to please God? Through modeling, demonstrating, teaching, discussion, setting the example through mentorship, and prayer. What are we modeling and living in front of our children? What are we teaching and how are we speaking into the lives of our children? In my own life with my son, it is imperative that he understand the importance of having an opinion, even more important, a sound opinion, and even in disagreement, to do so with respect and humility. It is in the tone and delivery.

So what should your relationship with your child look like? Does it change as he or she becomes older? Absolutely. As they enter the world and grow up right in front of our eyes in what seems like the flash of a second, begin by praying for and with your children. Your relationship with your children start before the womb as you begin to pray for your children's lives. You may feel this is premature, but if you desire to have children, the best gift you can give your child is a praying parent who can help to establish and develop their relationship in Christ. Pray as the Lord leads you to pray over various realms of their future life. When in the womb, do not be afraid to lay hands over your stomach and pray blessings over their lives and their children and future generations. Pray for the strength and wisdom of God to be the parents that God has called and destined you to be. Pray regarding your children's spiritual gifts and the development of their spiritual gifts, for your ability to spiritually recognize those gifts, promote those gifts to glorify God, and edify His kingdom. Pray God's protection over their spirit, their bodies-God's temple, their hearts, and their minds. Pray aloud as your child hears and begins to be comforted by his or her mother's voice and the voice of other loved ones who frequent your world.

One evening a few months ago, I was attending my son's "Back to School" night at his high school. A junior, "Can you believe it?" I thought. As we walked on campus, meeting this year's teachers, becoming reacquainted with teachers of the past, meeting his friends and their parents, I was taken aback by what I saw. I no longer saw this little toddler, or the middle schooler, I saw someone who is becoming a man before my very eyes. He is kindhearted, respectful, intelligent, confident, godly assertive, humble, a heart of mercy and generosity, and most importantly, a believer and follower of God, learning how to hear and recognize the voice of God and being obedient to God's instructions. He's the kind of young man who doesn't hang out at friends' homes; they all crash my house, instead. I don't mind, as I welcome it as he has a good group of friends. How did we get here? Through prayers, laying hands on my son, and through staying faithful in the Word. Am I the perfect parent? No, wouldn't pretend to be. But what I am is a praying momma. I started praying about how I can reward him for being...well, my son! Then it dawned on me. A praying parent is the best gift a parent can give their child. There are times when I'm up late writing, and he would have nightmares. I walk into his room, lay hands on his forehead, and pray over him to sleep peacefully. We make it a point to pray together every morning before he heads off to school. Be intentional about praying for and with your children. It's never too late nor is it ever too early to pray over your children.

For those who are believing God for children, pray for every realm of your future child's life. If you are expecting, lay hands over your stomach and pray blessings over your children and future generations. Pray for the strength and wisdom to be the parents God has called and destined you to become. Pray regarding their spiritual gifts, the development of those gifts, and for your ability to recognize and promote those gifts to glorify God and edify His kingdom. As your children get older, pray God's protection over their spirit, their bodies-God's temple, their hearts, and their minds. Pray over their circle of influence, meaning their friends, mentoring groups, their school, church youth groups, and your communities. My God, pray for the child who you want to come back to the Lord. May prayer, praise, and thanksgiving always be on our tongues concerning our children. God has entrusted us, so let us treat His treasures of children with grace, respect, and love.

What if your little ones are no longer little and they are living their best life as adults? I am sure your predictable response is, "Well, they will always be my baby," right? We see it often, and I am sure if you have college students, then you may have experienced the staff speaking primarily to your adult child, unless your college kid has given consent for staff to speak to you.

So what am I saying? Prayer is the first step in developing a sound relationship with your children, with Christ being the head of the parental relationship. Hopefully, you have reflected over time of the ideal relationship you want to have with your children in comparison to the actual relationship you have with them. Ask yourself what factors play a role in your parenting relationship? Where did you learn this type of relationship? Is it volatile? This is not a conversation coming from a judgmental place nor should you walk away from this expecting yourself to be perfect. No, allow this to be a check-in moment, an ah-ha moment, a moment of reflection when you genuinely ask yourself if your relationship with your children a reflection of God's love. Is your relationship with your children a reflection of your relationship with God? Hmmm, did that question stir something? I hope it did. When we look at our relationship with our children, it is a reflection of our relationship with God.

Example of a Parent's Love

A dear sister in Christ shared her experience with her children during a gals' lunch. She had three young kids at the time of her experience, and was raising them on her own. We were talking specifically about her style of parenting. She shared a story where she needed to make a decision that was going to impact their single female-headed household. The family needed to downsize and move into a more affordable home. Now, this indeed was a challenging decision because moving, as we know, may involve changing schools, friends, sports teams, and extracurricular activities, on top of the additional stress of moving itself. The thought crossed my friend's mind to complete the entire moving process without involving the children from looking, to eventually informing her kids, "Mom found a house, and we're moving on this particular date." She knew it was going to be some resistance as this was the home they were in prior to the divorce. It was inevitable that they move rather quickly. My friend decided to pray and fast for a short length for God's direction. Upon ending her fast, God led her to include her children in the entire process. She had a family meeting that evening, which she stated that she would hold on average, a bi-weekly or monthly basis. During this family meeting, this mom of two teens and a school-aged child sat down with her kids in the living room after dinner to explain in age-appropriate yet realistic terms that she was unable to afford their current place. She went on to say that home was where you make it. Prior to this meeting, she had time to individually process this situation, reflect on the conversation, how she would include the children in the conversation, and felt emotionally ready to have this conversation. This is not to say that you should not cry in front of your children, show emotion, or admit that you are nervous or scared, but within expressing emotion, it is important that your children feel secure in their relationship with you and in their knowing that God is in control. It was during the family meeting when my friend shared that although staying in their current home was a non-negotiable at this point, she presented areas where their voice would be taken into consideration. She further explained that she would make the final decision on items discussed, but that having her children's input was vital. She had explored various cities that would be close to her job and was generally within her budget. So she inquired out of the following two cities, "Which would you all like to see us move?" The kids took into account various factors, such as proximity to their current school, activities, and friends. She asked them whether they preferred a two-story house or a one-story house, and what were some must-haves, wants, and negotiables in the house that they would ultimately call home. When the kids did not agree, she allowed them to work out their disagreements while she provided guidance and clarity. Although it was evident that the family needed to relocate, she was insistent on incorporating the children in this major life-changing decision by providing the choices, hearing their voices, and making the final decision that God led her to take.

Some may be reading this and saying, "Oh no, there is no way that I would involve my kids in such an important decision," while others are saying, "I would not put my input or make the final decision, but allow my children to make all the decisions because it promotes free thinking and independence." What I hope you take from this story is that our children are individuals who need to learn the ability to one day function as adults. This is one of the primary goals in how they are going to be as adults. How are they going to make decisions? How are they going to live their lives? What type of jobs or careers will they take an interest in? What type of spouses are they going to marry if they decide that they desire marriage? How will they raise and parent your grandchildren if they decide to have children? My dear sister, you are a part of that equation. What you do today as a parent will have an impact on the type of people they become or not become.

Friends and Social Connections of Our Children

Do you know your child or teen's circle of friends? Do you know them by name? Okay, perhaps that question may be overwhelming, so allow us to examine one friendship. Can you describe one friendship of your child or teenager? What is his or her name? If we are referring to your teen, is this friend their boyfriend or girlfriend? Have you had conversations with their parent(s)? Do you know the parent(s)? Where do they specifically live? Have you been to their home? Have they been to yours? Have you observed and assessed the home environment of the individuals your child or teen calls a friend? Have you observed how your child interacts with their friend(s)? Have you observed changes, whether positive, negative, or indifferent in your child since being amongst this friend or group of friends?

I remember a time when friends invited me as a child to their home and my mother's response was, "I need to meet them first and get to know them." My parents, especially my mother, would never say yes immediately. Usually a yes would follow after a relationship had developed between my mother and their mother. An initial conversation would take place between our mothers, and rather than inviting only me, the parents would invite my parents to the home, and we would visit as a family. And when this did not occur, my mother would invite my friends and my brother's friends to our home. She would offer to pick them up and drop them off. This allowed an opportunity for my mother to become better acquainted with the child coming to their home. I was not aware of her intent until I became a mother. My parents, especially my mother, would observe any changes in my brother and I as we interacted with our friends. Were these positive or negative behaviors? How did our friends interact with their parents? Was it a respectful one with clear boundaries, and it was apparent that it was a parent-child relationship versus "my child is my friend" type of parental relationship. This continued into my teen years.

So imagine my surprise when my son reached the age when he asked to invite friends to our house. He informed me that he wanted his friend to come to our house after school and his friend's mother said yes. My immediate response was, "His mother said yes to what?" My son went on to say that he and his friend had a conversation with no discussion of details. I had not met the child nor his parents. So I requested the phone number of the mother, not the father, but the mother, to discuss plans. If you are wondering what this conversation looked like, it involved an informal introduction, how the kids met, and what each child had told each parent about the plan. As the hosting parent, I shared details of my schedule for the timeframe in question, my expectations, ensured the safety of my home, and who lives in the home with us. A little much for you, you may think. Yes, I am old school, and I believe in the importance of knowing who your children consider as friends.

Here is a tad bit of advice as I usually allow my teen's friends to visit our home as this allows me an opportunity to observe the interaction between my son and his friends. It gives insight as to the type of home environment they are raised in. And as time progresses, friends have become an extension of our family, including them visiting my parents' home for "Teen Saturdays" when the guys come over to my parents' for barbeque, games, and basketball. Having my son's friends over eventually led to it being the weekend hangout spot when on school breaks. I became the mother who would provide transportation, and sometimes, funds for the movies, amusement park, and other places that teens frequent. There were times when my family of two and our dog turned into a family of five or six teens spending the night, with them watching movies, playing board games, cracking jokes, and eating. Allowing his friends to come over has afforded the opportunity to develop motherly relationships with his peers, oftentimes opening the door for his friends to ask me for advice and for me to impart spiritual wisdom into their lives about dating, sex, school, career and academic aspirations, family, and other pertinent issues of this age. Yes, does this arrangement of being the hosting mother become interestingly challenging at times in the short term because it involves you having to possibly postpone plans, make sure your fridge is fully stocked, keep extra funds for a sudden pizza order, keep a functional space for the teens to do homework assignments or game playing, and a tidy place? In the long run, it should never be considered an inconvenience when you are investing in the lives of your children and their peers.

I remember two friendships, in particular, that started when my son was in middle school that dwindled over time as they entered their sophomore year. One friend who moved into the neighborhood spent much of his time alone with both parents working the day shift and graveyard, so he would spend many days and occasional nights at our home. I became better acquainted with his mother. My son would join them on birthday parties and the like. My son mentioned that his friend had several cousins their age involved in gang life. I shared with my son that I liked the young man, and he would always be welcome to our home, providing that he remained respectful, and his friend did not engage in gang activity or criminal activity as I did not want my son to have any association. As the months went by, his friend came over less and less, and my son mentioned him less. So one day, I asked my son what happened to his friend as I would see his friend in the neighborhood walking aimlessly. My son told me that he started to slowly drift away from his friend because his friend initiated into a gang. I do not have any ill feelings towards individuals who have chosen to join gangs. One feeling I am concerned of is oftentimes those becoming involved in the gang lifestyle do so for a sense of belonging and cohesion, a sense of having a mentor or someone to look up to, someone who understands them, and a sense of family, especially if their family of origin is not home often or present or there's a level of unhealthy or dysfunction in the home of origin. Having a basic understanding of this, I was heartbroken to learn of this news, and I continue to pray for this young man and his safety.

Another friendship of my son began in middle school and dwindled around the second semester of their sophomore year. I recall one Saturday evening, I drove my son and this friend to the movies, and I heard them speaking of his friend's girlfriend. Now, I am not a naïve mother as I knew that my son may have very well had a girlfriend, although my hope was that he would not engage in a romantic relationship until his college years when he was prayerfully more emotionally mature. His friend was sharing that he was going to "hang out" with his girlfriend. So me being the mother I am, I strategically placed myself in the conversation. Yes, comical, yet intentional. So as I found a parking space for them to get their belongings to head into the theater, I inquired about his relationship. He chuckled. My son, accustomed to my approach, comforted his friend by sharing, "Don't feel weird, my mom is like this with everyone, including me." His friend shared that he and his girlfriend kissed. I inquired further about whether the two were engaging in a sexual relationship, and if so, were they practicing safe sex, and if he spoke with his parents or if they were aware of the relationship. He assured me that they were not sexually active and further elaborated that his mother was aware.

This was where the topic of celibacy and abstinence came into the conversation and sharing the importance of purity and abstinence with our children. Likewise, letting our children know that in the event that they had already engaged in a sexual relationship or currently in one, it was not too late to turn a different path on their spiritual journey by choosing to abstain. As parents, some are afraid to have transparent conversations for fear that if we discuss sex, it will promote sexual relationships, or we assume that our children and teens are not talking about sex nor have the concern. News flash, moms! Our children, especially our teens, are aware of sex, and more than likely have conversations with their peers about sex or have a peer who is engaging in a sexual relationship, if not a sexual encounter. We live in the age of sexting, when minors send sexually explicit photos of themselves to peers or someone they may be interested in. Additionally, we live in a country where some schools provide forms of contraception, primarily condoms, located in the school office or nurse's office, without informing the parent. Legally, in some states, minors twelve years through seventeen may seek information about and obtain contraception, engage in some forms of medical treatment, and terminate a pregnancy without notifying the parent or legal guardian. This is a reality check and meant to encourage parents to be intentional in the conversations we have with our minors. It is more beneficial that our children receive information about sex from you or another trusted adult if you choose than a peer of theirs who does not have the wisdom and life experience to shed accurate light on this type of situation with your children.

During my continued conversation with my son's friend, it was revealed that he and his parents have a unique relationship where he was allowed to drink alcohol and experience certain drugs providing he was in the home with his parents at the time that he would engage in such behavior. Not wanting to overstep boundaries, but when God entrusted me as a parent for my son, my parenting wisdom and protection extends to my son's friends, and all children around me because the child's safety always comes first. I always informed his friends that I am always nearby for a listening ear for a word of wisdom or if they needed my support as they disclose certain topics with their parents. The young man moved in with various family members before returning to his parents' home, and most recently dropping out of high school. Again, heartbroken, as another child who would benefit from more direct guidance. My son disclosed that he slowly stepped away from this friendship because of the young man's involvement with drugs. When asked how my son responds to these types of relationships, incidences, and disappointments, he shared that he keeps them deep in prayer, but stopped hanging out with them.

As we discuss these types of incidences, it leads me to another question. What type of questions do you ask your children? What does your relationship look like Do your children feel comfortable discussing their friendships with you? When our children are little, we hold their hand, protect them by keeping them away from the bad and the evils of this world. Our job is to protect them and prevent them from engaging in anything considered dangerous or harmful. As our children become older, our parenting should evolve as well. With my son, I am no longer holding his hand as I did when he was two. Now, as the parent of a soon-to-be adult, my parenting approach and style have matured according to the needs of my son, who is almost an adult. Now, I am learning to step back and allow him to make age-appropriate decisions. Why? Because if I do not allow him to develop, to make age-appropriate reasonable mistakes while in my care, how is he going to develop the skills to address the challenges of life as a husband, father, and a man of God? It is a fine line and is difficult to bring ourselves to a place of peace and trust. We develop a trust of God within our children in knowing that we have raised them and equipped our children with the necessary tools to be successful God-fearing men and women of God. Now allow us to explore how we may be present and intentional in our children's lives while making a powerful God-fearing impact on their lives and in our world.

Present, Intentional, Impactful

As you read those words, what thoughts or feelings were evoked? In late 2018, I began praying about the series for our single mothers' ministry, and this was the first phrase that God spoke to me. I asked God to reveal His purpose behind these words and what they meant. As God revealed in weeks and months to follow, He began to go into detail by defining these terms and how these terms apply to every area of my life, including parenting. To be present means to be in the here-and-now, to embrace the moment that you are in, taking advantage of every moment given, and having the ability to recognize when a "present" moment is taking place. For instance, when having a conversation with my son, my goal is for both he and I to place our cell phones to the side (not checking text messages, emails, playing games, or responding to calls), television turned off, and both actively engaged, actively listening, and proactive in the dialogue taking place. My son has the habit of having his body turned in a different direction other than in my direction. So we turn our body towards each other and engage in eye contact to show respect and attention to the other that we are actively engaged in the conversation. Being present and "in the moment" involves being physically, emotionally, and cognitively engaged in the conversation. It may be difficult to do this at times, but when one does not appear engaged, the other calls that person on it. Be open and willing to take advantage of every opportunity to do so.

Intentionality follows a similar concept. Intentionality involves doing and engaging in activities on purpose and with purpose. What does intentionality look like, especially as it pertains to parenting? It looks like making purposeful choices. Making the purposeful choice to attend the optional back-to-school program when you have the choice to stay home because you are exhausted from a full day of work. It looks like taking advantage of every opportunity as a teachable moment or as a moment to dialogue and learn more about your child. For instance, my son and I have an active lifestyle with my full-time employment, my part-time employment, we both are involved in ministry and church life, extracurricular activities, and so we spend a considerable amount of time in the car. Why not use this time wisely, especially when en route to school, home, or to an extracurricular activity? On the days that I pick up my son from high school, I use that time to ask questions, lots of questions, and active listening. Not just yes or no questions as I learned quickly, but thought-provoking questions that result in my son critically thinking, analyzing, elaborating, and developing the ability to articulate and self-advocate. I ask questions to find out more of my child's life, his studies, his thoughts, his concerns, his worries, and more. It is not a time to judge or critique or criticize, but to get to know the heart of your child. For instance, when my son gets into the car upon picking him up, I immediately ask how his day went. With a teenager, especially teenaged boys, their responses are usually short, such as "good." I will usually ask him to elaborate. As a parent, you have to develop the ability to discern whether your child needs time to themselves to unwind from the school day. Some children may need an hour or so to unwind, and their responses may be more developed when you do speak. I will tell jokes, which oftentimes will enable my son to be receptive to a conversation with me. I ask questions about each class period by inquiring about new concepts learned, concepts that were a review from a previous class or from the previous year, conversations they had with their teachers and what was discussed, and any concerns that they may have regarding the class, the subject, or with a peer or teacher. I inquire of classwork assignments and whether he completed them during class. I inquire about homework assignments and the tools he needs to complete the assignments. Additionally, I inquire about quizzes and exams taken during the day and upcoming quizzes and exams. Additionally, I ask questions to complete an emotions check and thought check so I may properly assess how my child copes with problems. If I am being honest, my son becomes annoyed with these questions at times, but it shows him that we are a team, I am here to support him, advocate for him, and empower him; likewise, it allows him to know that I am proactive and desire to engage in his life so I take advantage of what time we have whenever we may have it. Do not only wait for these moments to engage, but intentionally carve out time throughout the day and week to connect with your child through quality time.

I remember years ago, my idea of intentionality was quality time. But my quality time meant going to museums, amusement parks, the movies, out to dinners, and although going to those places with my son was fun, I was under the impression that that was quality time, and as long as we were engaged in these activities, I was connecting with him. Until one day, God led me to ask my son what his version of quality time meant. What was my son's love language? How did he enjoy "quality time?" My son shared that although when he was younger, going to those places was fun, now that he is older, these places did not equate to quality time, but more so busy time. He further emphasized the importance of grabbing a bite to eat, such as buying pizza and watching his favorite shows for 30 minutes to an hour, and as long as we did this at least once a week on a Saturday or Sunday evening, he was happy. This meant quality time to him. Imagine my surprise when he told this to me. Now you understand what connection and conversation can mean between you and your child. Come to know and understand your child's love language. My son has learned how to articulate his ideas, and when he does, I inquire, I probe, to learn more. Learn your child. Your child may not necessarily spell out their desires because they may not know or may even think that you do not care. It is your job to read between the lines, observe, analyze, study your child.

Lastly, be impactful In everything you do, may it be parenting, may it be ministry, your job, or a passion of yours, know that it is not about you, but about those God has called you to serve, assist, guide, and mentor. When you keep this view in the forefront, you come to realize that every moment is an opportunity for growth, is a teachable moment, and a time to speak into the lives of others. Consider this. God called us as He entrusted us with the gift of mothering, may it be biologically, through adoption, or via a special mentoring relationship. What legacy do you desire to leave behind for your family or your community? Perhaps it is a legacy of wealth, a legacy of knowledge, wisdom, and mindset.

Teaching Children How to Resolve Conflict

It is important that we, as parents, not resolve all worries for our children, especially as they mature as middle schoolers into high school, but that we equip them to recognize when there is an issue and to discern how and who to speak with to assist them in coming to a resolution. As parents, we have to be able to determine what is appropriate for our maturing children to resolve versus an issue that we, as parents, step into and resolve. Yes, it is difficult to do because our innate nature is to nurture and protect our cub, but part of protecting and nurturing our children is to guide them and show them to recognize the voice of God and make wise decisions that come from developing a sound relationship with the One who created them. As parents, we must learn how to take a step back and allow our children to make certain age-appropriate decisions. I say age-appropriate because some tasks require us, as parents, to step in such as if there is a concern at school and your child has discussed it with the teacher (if older, such as in high school), or is being bullied at school, then this requires your follow-through and involvement as a parent. It is your job to advocate on behalf of your child with the teacher, faculty, and school administration. And when you become involved at this level, do your research as a parent. Be mindful not to make assumptions that your child behaved cor-rectly or incorrectly. Do your research by asking questions of the incidence, before and after, who was involved, and conduct your mini-investigation to ascertain the facts of the players before approaching the school or the parent. Again, we must conduct ourselves in decency and order, not in disarray, allowing our emotions to lead rather than rationality, poise, and godliness.

Practical Application

This chapter was filled with nuggets to apply within your life as parents. In this section, I'd like you to reflect on where you are in this parenting journey. This may be done by creating a visual by writing your responses, thoughts, and emotions to the following questions: Are you a single mother and have the pri-mary or complete parenting responsibility? Are you co-parenting with the father of your children? Are you one where the father may not be involved, but you have created a village of family, friends, and extended loved ones who play various roles in your child(ren)'s life? Are you a recent divorcee or recently single? Are you married and feel that the primary responsibility of parenting falls upon you, or perhaps you have an equal parenting relationship with your spouse or significant other? Maybe your children are now teens or now adults, and you have entered a new stage on this parenting journey. Not everyone's reality is your reality, but there are some concepts that we, as parents, may have in common regardless of the type of parenting and the stage that you are in.

Next, as you explore your parenting relationship, write down your views on parenting and how those views were established, perhaps through your personal experience growing up. What does your ideal parenting look like? What areas is your parenting strong in and what areas do you believe need improvement? Furthermore, develop strategies and time frames on how you plan on implementing these strategies. Perhaps you create a specific goal of attending a biblical parenting course at your church. You may have a goal of enrolling in a child development class online or at a local community college to learn about where your child or teen is developmentally, emotionally, physiologically, and cognitively. Maybe it is attending a workshop or seminar on an aspect of parenting, such as behavioral concerns or how to foster a relationship with your teen. It may even be attending a support group for parents raising children with special needs once monthly or quarterly. Growing and learning never stops, so know that there is always room to grow in every facet of life, especially parenting.

The next part of this exercise is to examine your home life, family life, and structure or level of consistency in your home. For two weeks, I would like you to keep a separate journal of your observations of your home. Do not mention to your children or anyone else in the home that you are observing and analyzing the flow of the home. Take note of the atmosphere in your home. Is your home littered with anger and pain, as evidenced by a lot of yelling, cursing with, and or in front of your children? Is it peaceful and quiet with little communication? How do your children communicate with each other? Pay attention to the television time and videogame time of children. Again, in this two week period you are not addressing any specific behaviors unless you observed physically harmful and emotionally damaging behavior. You are simply quietly observing and jotting down notes in your quiet time of situations, behaviors, or the such that you would like to discuss at the conclusion of this period. At the end of the two week period, and I would strongly suggest after you have completed all the exercises in this chapter's practical application, you hold a family meeting discussing your observations. If residing with your spouse or significant other, meet privately with them first and develop common ground before meeting with the family. Discuss areas of strength and areas where improvement is needed, the ultimate goals and hopes within the next several months and one year, and strategies to achieve them. Depending on your parenting style, you may include your children and others living in the home or village to develop family goals and strategies to achieve those goals and time frames. To make this a more powerful statement, create a board as a family project on family goals, time frames, and progress, and post it in a frequently traveled common area in the home where everyone may be reminded several times daily.

Now, allow us to explore the leadership and parenting style of your home. Review the leadership and parenting styles discussed earlier in the chapter. Which resonates most with you? Are they situational, meaning the style you express varies depending on the situation or depending on your child's personality? Evaluate your style and whether this parenting style aligns with the adult you aspire to see in your children years in the future.

Lastly, being present, intentional, and impactful are vital pieces to the growth of our children and the development of our relationships with them. List and elaborate on ways in which you are or hope to be present, intentional, and impactful in your children's lives. Know that parenting is a never-ending journey. It changes and evolves along the way, but nothing is etched in stone and may be up for improvement when the situation and time seem appropriate. We make mistakes as parents, we are not perfect. So when we make mistakes, repent to God, and apologize and have conversations with your kid when you, as a human being and as a parent, do something wrong and move forward. Yes, apologizing when you're wrong to your children shows transparency, humility, wisdom, and they develop a new level of respect, especially when you are sincere and vow to strive not to continuously make that mistake. Let us close this chapter by seeing how God guides us in His Word on our relationship with our children and the home God has called us to create for them.

Applicable Scriptures

"Fathers, do not exasperate your children: instead, bring them up in the training and instruction of the Lord" (Ephesian 6:4).

"The rod and reproof give wisdom, but a child left to himself brings shame to his mother" (Proverbs 29:15).

"Whoever spares the rod hates his son, but he who loves him is diligent to discipline him" (Proverbs 13:24).

"And these words that I command you today shall be on your heart. You shall teach them diligently to your children, and shall talk of them when you sit in your house, and when you walk by the way, and when you lie down, and when you rise. You shall bind them as a sign on your hand, and they shall be as frontlets between your eyes. You shall write them on the doorposts of your house and on your gates" (Deuteronomy 6:6-9).

"And how from childhood you have been acquainted with the sacred writings, which are able to make you wise for salvation through faith in Christ Jesus" (2 Timothy 3:15).

"But if a widow has children or grandchildren, let them first learn to show godliness to their own household and to make some return to their parents, for this is pleasing in the sight of God" (1 Timothy 5:4).

"Discipline your son, and he will give you rest; he will give delight to your heart" (Proverbs 29:17).

"As a father shows compassion to his children, so the Lord shows compassion to those who fear Him" (Psalm 103:13).

"Behold, children are a heritage from the Lord, the fruit of the womb a reward" (Psalm 127:3).

"Hear, my son, your father's instruction, and forsake not your mother's teaching, for they are a graceful garland for your head and pendants for your neck" (Proverbs 1:8-9).

"Fathers, provoke not your children to anger, lest they be discouraged" (Colossians 3:21).

"But as for me and my house, we will serve the Lord" (Joshua 24:15).

"Unless the Lord builds a house, the work of the builders is wasted" (Psalm 127:1a).

"Anyone who listens to My teaching and follows it is wise, like a person who builds a house on solid rock" (Matthew 7:24).

"You will be blessed when you go in and blessed when you go out" (Deuteronomy 28:6).

I hope this chapter truly ministered to your spirit. God has entrusted us with His most precious gift: children. Even in the most challenging moments, God knew that He created us with just the right temperament and love to raise them in the way He has called us to. Let us not take this monumental role for granted. Parenthood travels through seasons as with any other area in our lives. Sometimes it is pure bliss, other times we may be afraid that they are not ready for the real world, and then there are moments when we are looking for an apartment for them to move into at age sixteen 4,000 miles away because they have managed to strike the last nerve we have in our body. Hopefully, that made you smile. What about those of us who bear the unique responsibility of raising children on our own as single mothers? We will discuss this in the next chapter. In the interim, take some time to digest the nuggets in this chapter and when you are ready, let us go into prayer.

Prayer

Father, here I am, Lord. My home and the environment that I create for my family is not only a reflection of me, but primarily is a reflection of You. I vow to surrender myself, my home, and my family to You. Mothering is an important role, and I thank You for entrusting with the gift of parenthood. Reveal to me, Heavenly Father, Your will and Your choice in how we (you and God or you, God, and your significant other if the father is involved in parenting) should parent our child(ren). Bless me with Your wisdom and strength to be the parent You have called me to be and how to recognize opportunities for me to be present, intentional, and impactful in my child(ren)'s life. Show me how to implement appropriate and righteous structure in my home and most appropriate parenting style(s) for my child(ren). Lord, I trust You with my most prized possession, my children. Continue to equip me as I equip them in becoming the men and women of God You have called and destined them to become. In Jesus' name, we pray, Amen.

Chapter 5

I Am Mom And Dad Or Am I?

"There is therefore now no condemnation for those who are in Christ Jesus" (Romans 8:1).

HOW MANY OF US HAVE HEARD WOMEN SAY, "I am Mom and Dad" or "I have to be Mom and Dad" because their father is not here? Or maybe that woman is you? I can understand this point. Very early in my single-mothering journey, I believed this view and would often say it. But as I progressed through this journey for seventeen years, my view has changed tremendously. The tokens that are discussed in this chapter will help you on your journey of life and parenting. This chapter will contribute to developing a healthy view of the father of your child(ren). And it will help you to develop a healthy relationship with the father of your child(ren). Fostering a positive, safe, and healthy partnership is a helpful step toward achieving harmony in your life. If you are a single mother reading this, you may have mixed feelings about this, depending on your relationship with yourself, your relationship with the father of the child(ren), and the relationship you have with God. What was your relationship like with your father and the relationship between your father and mother? How did your mother interact with and perceived your father's role? Does that play a role in how you perceive your child(ren)'s father? Do you have a relationship with the father of your child(ren)? What does that relationship look like? Does that impact how you perceive your single-mothering experience and whether you see your role as mother and father?

When I finalized my idea on what I wanted to complete my doctoral qualitative study on, I decided to explore Christian single-mothering and how Christianity impacted their parenting. With the guidance of my dissertation chair and committee, I conducted a study that involved participant recruitment and interviews of several women who identified as local single Christian mothers. The participants were introduced into single motherhood through divorce, death of the child(ren)'s father, adoption, or as never-married women giving birth. Several findings were found through my qualitative grounded theory study after analyzing the data consisting of the initial demographic surveys and interviews. Several patterns or themes were found, specifically when investigating the intersection of Christianity, single-mothering, and parenting. One of the themes frequently reported was the relationship between the single mother and the father of the child(ren). Another theme observed in my findings were the impact of the relationship between the mother and child(ren)'s father on the mom's parenting. The type of co-parenting relationship, or lack thereof, was a contributing factor on how single mothers perceived single parenthood and their parenting. Participants who identified as having an unhealthy co-parenting relationship with the father of the children, whether the demise of the relationship occurred as a result of a divorce or as an unmarried couple, reported that single-mothering had its challenges and had different perspectives on parenting. However, those who had a positive relationship with the father of their children had a more positive parenting experience. Additionally, they reported having more positive emotional well-being compared to single mothers who had a negative relationship with the father of the children. Participants who reported having an unhealthy co-parenting relationship due to the added pressures of a stressful relationship with the father or when the father was not present due to death, reported having a less healthy emotional well-being; thus, having an impact on their parenting. Such factors that made the co-parenting relationship challenging was a high rate of domestic violence with the father of the child(ren), through never married or divorce, being the perpetrator. Parental alienation was observed as being a factor within the reported unhealthy co-parenting relationship. Why do I mention the findings of my study within this section? Because interestingly, those who had a less favorable and less healthy co-parenting relationship had a stronger propensity to state that they played the role of both mother and father. Whereas, the opposite was true for those who had a healthy co-parenting relationship.

I am passionate about this because we want to be careful with what we say. It is inappropriate and unhealthy to the child's well-being to demean, make less than favorable comments about the father of the child based on your feelings and your experiences. Allow your child to develop their view of their father. It may seem different from yours, but as time continues, the truth of the other parent will be revealed, whether positive or negative. There are exceptions to this view, including if there is history of harm or the potential of physical or psychological harm being caused to or around the child. In this case, you must do what is legally appropriate to protect your child.

Allow us to explore the role of father and mother, husband and wife, biblically. When you think of the role that a woman plays as a mother, what does that look like? What thoughts, feelings, and emotions are evoked? When we review Scripture upon Scripture, there are countless references to mothers and motherly-like characteristics that women are encouraged to embody.

For example, when we read of Mary's relationship with Jesus, it was one of admiration, selflessness, nurture, compassion, and respect. Despite what others may have said when she was told that she was going to birth the Messiah, imagine the stigma of being an unwed pregnant woman. Yet, she believed God. She was trusted, trustworthy, and faith-filled, and allowed herself to be a vessel for God's hope, light, and promise to the world to be manifested in human form. Let us consider Jochebed, the mother of Moses, who was self-sacrificing, selfless, and innovative to do what needed to take place as a mother to ensure that her son's life was saved. She gave birth to Moses, and when it was revealed that Pharaoh had commanded that all male Hebrew children born would be killed, it was Jochebed who placed her sweet boy in an ark and concealed the ark along the riverbank. She prayed and sought God's guidance as she implemented a plan for her dear Moses to be discovered by Pharaoh's daughter. Jochebed suddenly appeared and presented herself to Pharaoh's daughter as a nursing woman willing to nurse the child until Moses was of weaning age, at which time Pharaoh's daughter would raise him as her own. Can you conceptualize the magnitude of this act of faith and selflessness to God? She sacrificed her own feelings of knowing that she would one day leave him permanently in the household of Pharaoh. She sacrificed the possibility of being discovered to save her son's life. Another example of a mother's character is Hannah, one of the two wives of Elkanah and mother of Samuel in the Book of First Samuel. She was the true testament of faith and servanthood. Despite years of trying to conceive and desiring to conceive a child, she remained barren. Her sister wife would mock her for what seemed to be the inability to bear children as motherhood and fertility were the sign of true femininity and womanhood. One day, she found herself in the presence of God in a posture of worship, humility, and grace. She praised God to the point where others thought she was drunk. She was not drunk with wine, she was drenched in the Holy Spirit, knowing that God had a word for her, believing that her prayers were to manifest. She promised God that she would give her son back to Him. She conceived and bore Samuel, and when he was of an appropriate age, she gave Samuel back to God by allowing him to permanently serve God in the house of God, where he would develop the ear to hear when the Lord spoke. Out of obedience, loyalty, and strength, she gave her son, the one God blessed her with, back to Him. Have you considered Naomi in the Book of Ruth? Ruth was one of Naomi's daughters-in-law. Naomi was married and gave birth to two sons. Both sons married and with their wives lived with Naomi and their father in a foreign land until Naomi's husband died, followed by the death of her two sons. She and her daughters-in-law were the surviving kin, without any children of their own. Naomi gave the opportunity to leave her so they may move forward with another husband while still in their youth. One daughter-in-law left, but Ruth stayed with Naomi, vowing to go where Naomi went and serve whom Naomi served. Naomi was a mother figure to Naomi, proving to be an older woman of wisdom. Naomi served in the capacity of mentor, guide, and a voice of discernment. This picture hopefully encapsulates every facet of mothers. There are several examples within the Bible of the sacrificial love of a mother.

What about the role of a father and Scriptures supporting this? What thoughts and emotions are evoked when you think of the role of a father? How did you see your parents? Were there other couples in your life who resembled what you feel is an exemplary example of father and mother roles? What about now? Are there individuals who you believe are great examples of what you envision as a godly mother and godly father?

My hope is that you would come to understand in reading this text that a woman is unable to play the role of mother and father just as a single father is unable to play the role of a mother and father. God created you and entrusted you with your children and equips you with the tools, providing that you accept to be the best mother He has created and designed you to become. Men and fathers are biblically and in society, seen as the provider. Women and mothers, in particular, are perceived as nurturers, more emotionally and spiritually in tune and the primary caretaker, and tending to the sensitive needs of others, especially their children. When the father is not involved or demonstrates little involvement, and the mother is the primary provider, especially financially, she may tend to diminish the role of the father to the financial provider.

Now, some may read this text and react with an angry tone, saying that this view is "old fashioned," "old school," or perhaps Old Testament versus New Testament. May we not add to the Word or take away from it as it is the living Word of God, and is the same yesterday, today, and forevermore.

What I hope you take away from this chapter is how you and the father of your children co-parent. Additionally, exploring how this relationship impacts how you parent your children, how you speak of your children's father, both in private and with your children, and how to improve the co-parenting relationship. While there are different dynamics, may it be a healthy co-parenting relationship, a single mother bearing complete responsibility with little to no involvement from the father, or an alternative family household; we, as women, were not created to be the father or father figure. He created us in our own beauty, femininity, wisdom, strength, and insight to be mothers to the children in our lives. This does not make us the spiritually weaker vessel, less than, or inferior to our male counterparts. It gives us the ability to work in connection and accord with one another to raise children in the way the Lord has entrusted us to do so. This is not an easy task, especially for those who have an unhealthy relationship with the father of their children. This involves prayer, support of spiritual, tangible, and professional means, and resources to move in godly wisdom.

Practical Application

In this exercise, explore your views on the role of the mother and of the father. Think about this in terms of both biblical and practical. How do you perceive the relationship between you and the father of your children? What is the relationship between your children and their father? Now, perception and reality may be different. How is the actual relationship between you and the father of your children and the relationship between your children and their father?

Applicable Scriptures

"These commandments that I give you today are to be on your hearts. Impress them on your children. Talk about them when you sit at home and when you walk along the road, when you lie down and when you get up. Tie them as symbols on your hands and bind them on your foreheads. Write them on the doorframes of your houses and on your gates" (Deuteronomy 6:6-9).

"The righteous man walks in his integrity: his children are blessed after him" (Proverbs 20:7).

"As a father has compassion on his children, so the LORD has compassion on those who fear him" (Psalm 103:13).

"My son, do not despise the Lord's discipline, and do not resent his rebuke, because the Lord disciplines those He loves, as a father the son he delights in" (Proverbs 3:11-12).

"Then I said to you, "Do not be terrified; do not be afraid of them. The Lord your God, who is going before you, will fight for you, as he did for you in Egypt, before your very eyes, and in the wilderness. There you saw how the Lord your God carried you, as a father carriers his son, all the way you went until you reached this place" (Deuteronomy 1:29-31).

"Fathers, do not exasperate your children; instead, bring them up in the training and instruction of the Lord" (Ephesians 6:4).

"And he passed in front of Moses, proclaiming, "The Lord, the Lord, the compassionate and gracious God, slow to anger, abounding in love and faithfulness, maintaining love to thousands, and forgiving wickedness, rebellion and sin. Yet he does not leave the guilty unpunished; he punished the children and their children for the sin of the parents to the third and fourth generation" (Exodus 34:6-7).

"Children are a heritage from the Lord, offspring a reward from him. Like arrows in the hands of a warrior are children born in one's youth. Blessed is the man whose quiver is full of them. They will not be put to shame when they contend with their opponents in court" (Psalm 127:3-5).

"But if serving the Lord seems undesirable to you, then choose for yourselves this day whom you will serve, whether the gods your ancestors served beyond the Euphrates, or the gods of the Amorites, in whose land you are living. But as for me and my household, we will serve the Lord" (Joshua 24:15).

"Start children off on the way they should go, and even when they are old they will not turn from it" (Proverbs 22:6).

These Scriptures speak to the respect and honor that we hold mothers to:

"Treat older women as you would your mother, and treat younger women with purity as you would your own sisters" (1 Timothy 5:2).

"She opens her mouth with wisdom, and loving instruction is on her tongue. She watches over the ways of her household, and does not eat the bread of idleness" (Proverbs 31:26-27).

"Her children arise up, and call her blessed; her husband also, and he praises her" (Proverbs 31:28).

"The aged women likewise, that they be in behavior as become holiness, no false accusers, not given too much wine, teachers of good things; That they may teach the young women to be sober, to love their husbands, to love their children, to be discrete, chaste, keep at home, good, obedient to their own husbands, that the word of God be not blasphemed" (Titus 2:3-5).

"She is clothed with strength and dignity; she can laugh at the days to come" (Proverbs 31:25).

"There are many virtuous and capable women in the world, but you surpass them all" (Proverbs 31:29).

"Listen, my son, to your father's instruction, and don't reject your mother's teaching, for they will be a garland of grace on your head and a gold chain around your neck" (Proverbs 1:8-9).

"Please, my Lord," she said, "as sure as you live, my Lord, I am the woman who stood here beside you praying to the Lord. I prayed for this boy, and since the Lord gave what I asked Him or, I now give the boy to the Lord. For as long as he lives, he is given to the Lord." Then he bowed in worship to the Lord there" (1 Samuel 1:26-28).

This chapter is again about a paradigm shift. It may have stepped on some toes because it encouraged you to have an out-of-the-box perspective. We live in a culture that at times focuses heavily on downgrading men and downplaying their efforts. As a single mother reading this book, the hope is by understanding the role of the father or father-figure in your children's lives, you will open your heart, mind, and spirit to the possibility and need to partner with the father in this journey called parenthood. In some cases, it is understandable that it may not be such a clear-cut situation, and other contributing factors play a role, but if it can be done safely and healthfully, let us work together. Marking a distinction between your feelings towards the father of children as a former lover and the father of your children. Truly ponder on that sentence. It is about having a paradigm shift. What is your worldview when it comes to single- mothering? What is your mindset as you move through this journey? Well, allow us to delve into a few in the next chapter.

Prayer

Heavenly Father, remove from my spirit any and all unhealthy thoughts, resentment, unforgiveness, animosity towards the father of my child(ren). Give me Your strength to be the woman of God and mother of God You have destined and designed me to become. Bless me with grace on how to understand my calling of motherhood and work, move, and walk in that anointing. Thank You for equipping me to move in this role of motherhood. Amen.

Chapter 6

The Mentality of a Woman

"Whatever you do, work at it with all your heart, as if working for the Lord, not for human masters" (Colossians 3:23).

THE MINDSET THAT YOU HAVE AS A SINGLE parent sets the precedence for the type and quality of a parenting experience you will have. Are you holding onto unhealthy ways of looking at life? Do you struggle with interweaving identity with the role of motherhood without separation of the two? Is your identity wrapped into the various tasks that you engage in? Is there a codependence between you and someone else such as a friend, family member, or your children? We are not meant to be a crutch, an enabler, or hindrance, but a help, a blessing, an advocate, and an uplifting voice to those who walk with you and those who are coming behind you. Is there a sense of mistrust and you have intentionally or unintentionally allowed that mistrust to impact the decisions that you make or the relationships you are involved in? Am I tapping into your core at this very moment? I am requiring you to dig deeper so that you can achieve harmony in your life.

Superwoman Mentality

What feelings are evoked when you read the heading *Superwoman mentality*? What does the Superwoman syndrome look like for you? Allow me to illustrate this mindset in the following example:

It's Friday morning, you are up at 5 a.m. to put in a quick load in the wash and finish those cupcakes that you promised for your 6-year-old daughter's classroom bake sale. You had hopes of having a quick moment to yourself with a cup of coffee, write your to-do-list for the day, and prayer time. But before you do, you sneak to your bathroom for a 5-minute shower. As you throw on your nursing scrubs for your full-time day job, your 6-year-old walks into your room, rubbing her eyes, ready to start her day. Then your 7-year-old calls for you from her room. You realize, like any other day, that "quick moment" disappeared just as quickly as the thought came. You use this time to get your girls dressed, teeth brushed, and ready for school. As they run downstairs to eat breakfast, you soon realize that you forgot to put the toast on, and now you smell a burning odor coming from your oven. Your daughter's cupcakes! Or shall I say, burnt biscuits, no longer edible. You glance at the clock as you wave smoke towards the kitchen window. It is 7:25, ten minutes past the time you all should have left. The girls grab their bags, you slap some sandwiches together, grab two apples, granola bars, and apple juice, throw it in a lunch pail, and the three of you run to the car, headed towards the store down the street for two dozen cupcakes. The girls attend two different schools across the street from each other. They both manage to make it to school by the bell as their teachers, who know your last-minute routine to the tee, ran to your car to retrieve them, and as you drop off your-seven-year-old, the teacher closes the car door, and then pokes her head in the window and ask you to volunteer to be the PTA president. You are running late as normal, and really, your only thought is to get to work, so you said yes as you are not looking at it as another commitment that you do not have time for, but as an investment for your children. You speed off and arrive at work twenty minutes late, but ten minutes before your usual late arrival time.

Your workday as a nurse ends. You pick up your first grader in the daycare held at the school before you pick up your oldest in the afterschool program a few minutes before they close at six. You manage to work an evening job as a bookkeeper at a warehouse five nights a week. You catch up with your girls during the half-hour drive to your friend's home so she can watch the kids while you work a few hours at your nighttime job. By ten at night, you are carrying two sleeping children up to their rooms. Fifteen minutes later, the girls are tucked into bed. And now you're responding to the reading discussion questions for your online bachelor's program in nursing.

Are you exhausted reading this scenario? To think, there are women who are living this life for years at a time. This scenario may remind you of yourself or someone you know. This was very much similar to my life in different seasons.

The Superwoman mentality is best described as one who does not feel that she needs help or may not like asking for help from others. This is very different from not having the resources and support system to ask for help resulting in functioning in survival mode. It may include not realizing or understanding the power of saying no. It may involve a mindset that by admitting you require help suggests that you are somehow weak, deficient, not a woman, or cannot handle your own or manage your life or household well. This is simply not true. It is a hectic lifestyle and can oftentimes leave you emotionally depleted. So if this describes you or how you interact with others, let us explore the source behind this lifestyle. It stems from an unhealthy mindset of possibly wanting to seek approval and appease others, of not wanting to feel guilty, or overcompensating, as we will discuss shortly.

I will share my experience as a *Superwoman* mom. As mentioned previously, months after I graduated with my doctorate, I was offered a position as a part-time college instructor. I applied in early February, had two phone interviews, a teaching demonstration, and by mid-March, I was attending orientation. Around the same time, I was offered a position in leadership. I was in my fourth year of leading the single mothers' ministry, and my son was in his sophomore year of high school. In the midst of working long hours at my day job and extensive hours at my part-time, I gained fifteen pounds in six months, tipping the scale of diabetes type two, frequent headaches, a recurring back injury, and random trips to urgent care. I was getting an average of five hours of sleep nightly, and quite frankly, was running on fumes, wondering why the weight that seemed to have occurred overnight was not dropping. In between my son's taekwondo, mentorship program, his tutoring sessions, and his volunteering, I found myself running on fumes trying to find balance and structure. I had functioned on a level of high stress for so many years that I had reached a new level of normalcy. It was normal for me to not have time to myself. It was normal for me to do it all; however, the difference was that I had the physical support of my parents and younger brother if I found myself in a jam.

At times, I allowed my pride to step in and keep me from being my best self. On one occasion, I remember driving 45 minutes from one job to pick my son up from school by our home only to venture the 45 to 60 minutes back to work, resulting in low productivity, more gas, less time, and poor efficiency. Does that make sense to you? Me neither. I can recall my father having a talk with me, saying, "Chanel, we live in the neighborhood right next to yours. I'm retired, it does not make sense for you to do this unnecessary driving when I'm right around the corner and can pick him up for you." What a lifesaver! In the midst, God was showing me that I was not alone and God positioned me in that moment, in that season, to have the additional support. I would be remiss to not be receptive. God revealed that it was deeper than that, but I had an issue of mistrust. I had developed the view that if I did not have expectations of others, I could not be disappointed if they failed to show up the way I needed. It was a purging and healing that needed to take place. It was a heart issue that was manifesting in how I navigated through life, how I made decisions, and how I functioned in my daily routine.

We should always be in a place of self-reflection and awareness. Evaluate where you are in life, your mindset, shifts in your views, and adjust as God leads. How is this mindset, my lifestyle, and lack of needing, wanting, or asking for help impacting our family? At some point, we have to grow in our spiritual maturity and be vulnerable with God. God is wanting us to live our best lives in complete God confidence. It requires vulnerability, so He may reveal what needs healing, restoration, and redemption.

If you identify as being a Superwoman, allow us to explore deeper. Underneath being a former self-proclaimed Superwoman was a status that I was proud of when I searched deep within my soul. As I was maturing into my late teens and young adulthood, I discovered this need to want to appease, to want to be validated, contributed to a level of poor self-image. This worsened as I moved through my twenties and thirties until I allowed God to remove the covering of deceit off my eyes. So let us go even deeper. The more I became involved in various activities and tasks and roles, the less I felt I needed help, and the more validated I felt that I became. Somehow, societal, and especially cultural pressures, and in some cases, family influences, can make a woman feel that she is less than when asking for help. "Less than," you ask? Less than a woman because, after all, a woman is made to accomplish everything on the list and then some. Less than a mother because, after all, mothers are nurturers and are created to tend to every need of everyone before her own, and that is if she has time to tend to self-care. The less than approach is a lie that we have allowed ourselves to believe.

Have you heard of the nature versus nurture argument? The nature versus nurture argument speaks to whether behaviors and physical manifestations expressed occur as a result of one's genetic make-up or DNA, or if one's behaviors are nurtured. In other words, cultivated or socialized, and are a result of how one is taught and who is within their micro and macro spheres of influence. Are women natural caretakers? Possibly. Are women cultivated and socialized to take care of and tend to the needs of others? Again, possibly. Regardless of where you fit on this spectrum, there remains one point. Has the concept of self-care been brought into the conversation? It is important to recognize and embrace our limits and boundaries. Being aware of those limits does not make you any less of a woman or weak. Self-awareness makes you strong, powerful, and dare I say it-human. It is important to recognize when we feel overwhelmed and overextended, and is it a choice, an unconscious response, or perhaps pridefulness of knowing a more healthy way to live life and choosing not to?

Survival Mode Mentality

I know this type all too well. What about you? It is common, and you may especially see this occur among single mothers. It occurs when the behaviors you express, the mindset in which you experience life, the tasks and activities you engage in are coming from a place of "doing what I have to do," the "it is what it is and I have to get it done," and "If I don't do it, it won't get done." Unlike the Superwoman syndrome, when one may have a support system or opportunities for assistance and chooses not to utilize that help, the survival mode speaks to those who do not have help. For the woman working from a survival mindset, it may involve not having a support system and having the feeling of needing to rely primarily on herself to provide for her family physically, spiritually, emotionally, and in some cases, financially. Similar to the Superwoman syndrome, one may find themselves existing, not living, and working off of fumes of exhaustion and emotional depletion compared to a place of rejuvenation and healthfulness.

Overcompensation Mentality

You may question what overcompensation may be referring to, so allow me to explain this further. Have you seen an individual who engages in various activities, and at times, activities that may be considered addictive in nature, as an intentional or unintentional way to make up or replace the lack of something? For instance, you may examine your life as a parent and engage in an activity that would essentially make up for that time or area of lack. This could be the lack of time, lack of money, lack of a father in the home, lack of quality time, lack of resources or support, for instance.

I have had seasons where God revealed to me that I was overcompensating. I recall the lavish birthday parties for my son that I needed to forego paying several bills for or engaging in higher-end items and events for my son. I'll give an example; several years ago, I wanted to throw my son a huge birthday party, and as a matter of fact, I would throw one yearly until I realized what I was doing. One year, I decided to throw my then eight-year-old son a birthday party. We invited approximately forty people. This included my friends with and without children, friends who no longer had young children, family, and my son's friends. I purchased the highest package and purchased additional food and items for all attendees. Yet, borrowed money from friends to pay my utilities and for other necessities that month and a couple months after. Now, let me preface by saying that there is no wrongdoing in lavish parties, birthday parties for your children, or similar because it is important to celebrate the ones we love and to celebrate ourselves too. There is nothing wrong with investing in the lives of those we care about. But what is the motivation behind the action or behavior? That is what I want you to ponder. I see this behavior oftentimes amongst single mothers who intentionally want the best for their children, but unintentionally overcompensate for the lack of perhaps the father being emotionally and or physically present, so perhaps they continuously go outside their means and outside of their budget, or continuously overextend themselves to the point of exhaustion and emotional depletion. Perhaps it is to lower your standards or expectations, becoming more laxed in your parenting style, or not providing a more structured and less disciplined environment to compensate for not being home as often because you work multiple jobs. Again, what is the motivation behind your actions and the mindset and emotions that accompany? It is well to have events, ascertain items, go above the norm, at times, for resources, or to reward your children, but doing so at the expense of putting the livelihood of your home at risk or your emotional and overall well-being in danger is questionable.

I recall one of many seasons of working multiple jobs simultaneously. For most of my adulthood, I have worked multiple jobs at the same time while working on my graduate degrees. When my son was younger, I made an extra effort to travel to museums, fairs, restaurants, and events throughout California and Phoenix, and Arizona on the weekends. There were times when we arrived an hour before the place closed. Some places involved a considerable amount of money, although for a short time for entrance fees, parking, and travel time and expenses. My intent was pure as I wanted to spend quality time with my son, but as my son entered his adolescent years, the less he wanted to visit museums and the like. Granted, it is common for children of this age to spend less frequent quality time with their parents. The more I worked multiple jobs, worked on my degrees, the more I spent a considerable amount of time away from home during the day and some evenings. Other nights, I was physically home, but not all the time emotionally present when working on a dissertation. As I went into prayer on how to resolve time constraints, God revealed the reality that I was overcompensating for there not being a father in the home, for me not being married, for me not being as physically and emotionally present.

One day, I had a conversation with my son. After praying together, we went into a long discussion of our home, our family, and the changing dynamics of our parenting relationship. Although our children may not know what they need in certain situations as they are growing and evolving through trial and error, do not take their voices away. Do not take their voices for granted. I knew that as my son became older, I could no longer hold his hand like I did when he was three. Now, I needed to evolve because our parenting relationship was evolving, and I needed to allow him space and time to grow and come into his own person, identity, and man. Our conversations were no longer of me making decisions for him, but me stepping back and allowing him to analyze and make age-appropriate decisions for himself. I provided opportunities to advocate for himself. I was there to offer guidance and be involved in decisions that pertained to school, career paths, friendships, and situations that involved the well-being of himself and his friends. During my conversation, I explained my intent and my desire to be the best mom that God had called me to be. I asked questions pertaining to his assessment of our parental relationship, his likes and preferences, dislikes, areas of improvement for him as a son, and for me as a mom. We discussed what his love language was as a child, and God showed me a valuable lesson during this conversation. My love language is quality time, so that meant that I receive love, and one of the most effective ways for someone to show me that they care is to spend quality time with me during an activity or going somewhere special. With this in mind, taking my son to various places was my way of showing that I cared for him and it was my way to express love for my son. My son said, "Mom, I don't need all of that." At first, I was appalled, but I quickly removed my feelings from the situation, placed them in my back pocket, and listened to my son's heart. The lesson that God was showing me was simply because my love language is quality time, did not mean that quality time is the love language for my loved ones and all those around me, including my son. I needed to hear the heart of the other individual and express love in the way they received it.

My son shared that he appreciated me saying *I love you* as I frequently had, but he was fine with us grabbing a pizza Saturday nights and watching his favorite show for an hour, and he was good until the following week for our next hangout time. I thought to myself, wow, that is pretty simple, and I can do that. Granted, there is more interaction during the week through daily conversations and check-ins, but this was definitely doable.

Why do I share this with you? How does this personal story relate to overcompensation? My prayer is that as you explore your mindset and as you begin to evolve to the next level of thinking, you will explore how you interact, respond, and react to those around you. How do you receive love, and how do you express love towards others, especially those closest to you? Sometimes, in the midst of doing what we feel is best is not what people need nor how they need to receive it in order for it to be most effective for them. Be open to the daily life lessons. God is so good and so amazing. Remember that as you evolve and move into a new paradigm, you are being molded into the vessel that

God has created you to be. Remember, He has entrusted your children to you. It was not by mistake, and it is never too late to allow God to move through you.

Help

As you reflect upon your own life, explore whether you can identify with overcompensating, survival mode, or having the Superwoman mentality. You may find that you identify with certain aspects of each mentality discussed. Is there one that you identify with more? Perhaps you notice that you experience aspects of one or more of the aforementioned during certain situations or when around certain people. Engage in introspection. As we have discussed with previous concepts, it requires a paradigm shift. Observe and analyze your thoughts, feelings, behaviors, and spirit. Analyze your current environmental situation, how you respond or possibly react to situations, and your support system. Do you have a support system? By a support system, I am referring to having a network of individuals whom you trust, can rely on, are loyal, supporting and encouraging, and people who believe in a two-way relationship. This group you may consider as your family, through blood or through friendship, is comprised of individuals who may offer various forms of support. This type of support includes two of three discovered during my study findings: tangible support and emotional support. This circle of support is a bond and friendship that is a two-way street, where you both give and receive, where each help and support one another. Tangible support may include forms of physical assistance, such as childcare, perhaps transportation, financial support, and other similar resources. Emotional support may include someone providing non-clinical advice or you needing encouragement, advice and suggestions, and someone to listen while you emotionally release stressors in your life. First, ask questions of whom out of the circle you consider as reliable. Does the individual share a similar belief system and similar values as you? Do they have similar parenting styles and disciplinary system? This occurs over time of observation and being in friendship with this person. Before having this conversation of requesting help, first, take it to God and examine your own life. Examine every area of your life, including your career, your family, your health, and decisions within your home where changes need to occur. Through prayer and conversation with God, He may reveal that you need to rearrange tasks, activities, and situations in your life to accommodate the changes that need to be made. There are other items to consider when you have sought guidance from the Lord on how to move forward, and you have received heavenly unction to seek help and support from your circle. This includes allowing an opportunity for your friend or family member to discuss your request of help with their spouse as they need to be on one accord prior to making a decision that would impact their home, home schedule, or the structure of their home, even if appearing minimal.

Perception of Others

Perhaps it is not an issue of not having help or a support system. It may be a concern of not understanding the power of saying no. What is the underlying root to you not saying no or a no that you stand by? Is it a fear or desire to not offend others? To not hurt the feelings of others? It is your desire to please and appease others? Is there concern that it will tarnish your reputation or perhaps tarnish the image that you believe others have of you?

Perhaps we need to delve into this concept more, the underlying source of not wanting or feeling as though you do not have the ability to say no. The reality is fear is the underlying source related to poor self-image and poor confidence. The reality is NO is a complete sentence. No is the beginning and the end. No does not need to come with an explanation after or a disclaimer before. No does not need to come with a certain tone or a passive gesture, such as looking down or avoiding eye contact. No does not need to come with behavioral changes where you avoid the individual via in person or on the phone. It is important to understand your limitations and establish boundaries around that. As you develop in your relationship with God, allow Him to reveal areas within your heart that require healing and restoration. Become vulnerable with God so He may help to break down walls that need to be broken and mend relationships and pieces that require healing.

A few years ago, I was sitting in class. We had just arrived to class, and our professor liked to begin each class with an exercise meant to relax us from the day and release any anxiety. It was a small class of about seven students. She dimmed the lights and asked us to sit completely still without any part of our body being crossed with both feet flat on the ground and arms rested on our lap or table. She asked us to think of the most difficult part of our day, such as an argument or a difficult situation at work, and immediately release it from our spirit, hearts, and minds from that moment forward. She followed by asking us to close our eyes, learn to pay attention to her voice, and be in tune with our body and our breathing at that moment. We were guided as she would name parts of our body, starting with the top of head. We were encouraged to focus on that part of the body, releasing any pain that needed to be released. She moved to the neck, shoulders, limbs, and all the way down to the feet, focusing on the body part she would name. Our professor began to describe a serene moment. And during this one occasion, I began seeing an image of me wearing an all-white dress walking towards a lush garden similar to what we may imagine of what the garden of Adam and Eve looked like. As I approached the entryway of this garden with a floral decorated awning, a man glowing in an all-white gown was standing ready to escort me in. Isn't that just like Jesus? As you draw close to Him, He will draw nearer to you. As I walked down the stairs, Jesus gently grabbed my hand and led me through the endless garden. My eyes rested upon the unique flowers, plants, and exotic colors. There were vivid colors that were unexplainable in our human language. As I walked through this garden being led by Jesus, I could smell the aroma of these unique specimens of life. As I walked through the garden, an overwhelming sense of love and peace fell upon me. This was the love of God that I felt in my spirit. Jesus walked me to a peaceful spot in the middle of this lush boundaryless garden. I had so many questions, questions upon questions, and had little time to ask as I was in awe, yet felt so comfortable because I was in the presence of a Heavenly Fatherly love. He did not provide time for me to ask questions because it was my time to listen. I did not speak, but Jesus was listening from my heart as I needed His guidance to keep going. Jesus whispered in my spirit, "My daughter, you are used to being in control, but it is time for you to be vulnerable and surrender to Me. Allow Me to lead you. Allow Me to guide you, and I will take care of you." I instantly knew what He was referring to as I needed to fully surrender in *ALL* areas of my life.

It was at that time that I began to slowly hear the voice of my professor encouraging us to slowly become physically and physiologically present. Jesus and I stood, and Jesus began leading me back up the stairs. But this time, I did not compartmentalize Jesus. I did not leave Him in the garden. Now, He was leading me outside of the garden. In my life, God was showing me that I had placed Him in a box awaiting to access Him when, if, and how I needed Him, not allowing Him to lead me. I needed to be in a place of quiet to hear His voice clearly. This moment was the beginning of a new season. It was the beginning of a para-digm shift.

So with this said, sister, it is time. Time for what, you may ask. Time to take off the cape. The cape of shame, the cape of guilt, the cape of overcompensation, pride, the cape of control and do-it-yourself because no one is going to do it better than you mindset. It is making a conscious intentional decision to choose to remove the cape for your peace and sanity so that you may present yourself in your world in the most healthy and functional way. It is time for change to occur in the natural and for physical manifestations of the paradigm shift as that may take time as you move through this process.

Remove the Cape

In reading signs of each type of situation, it is important to understand that each of us may flow in, out, and through each in any given period of time in our lives for any length of time. How well you persevere through each is the vital lesson to learn here. There is a process to change the mindset that under-lies each situation above. Three were highlighted in this sec-tion. Through your prayer and commune time with God, He may reveal other types of situations more tailored to you. As with many concepts that we discussed in this book, it begins with a paradigm shift-a shifting of the lens of how you see, and how you perceive the world around you, and how you choose to interact with others and respond. There are several situations that may not be detailed here, but it starts the conversation of how we, as women, mothers, wives, ministry leaders, and volun-teers show up and exist in this world. Why we do the things we do, how we interact with those in our environment, and how to create a healthier more authentic fearless self? Once you under-stand the power of saying no, you may be able to recognize when they are overextended, and how to implement strategies that promote self-preservation, and most importantly, God preservation in our lives.

So allow us to discuss strategies and applying those strategies in your life. During this process, a sense of God confidence develops, which leads us into our next section, the woman whom we hear often in the Christian world, the *Proverbs 31* woman.

Proverbs 31 Woman

The Proverbs 31 woman is where we will begin our conversation on developing a healthy God identity, lifestyle, and mindset shift. If you are a woman of faith, I am sure that you have heard of the Proverbs 31 woman, perhaps in women's Bible studies, conferences, or through your own personal time with God. Allow us to read and study line upon line, and identify key characteristics of the Proverbs 31 woman. This is not to say that you must exhibit every trait in the exact likeness or expression of the woman described in the Bible, as God will tailor to the unique way that He has created you.

As you remove the cape, remove the unhealthy mentality, remove the fear, and begin walking in faith, I encourage you to take a deeper look at Proverbs 31. The Proverbs 31 woman is the model that Christian women have been encouraged to aspire to be and the type of woman that Christian men have been instructed to base the choosing of their future wife on. God created us to embody certain traits. Some come with time, with life experience, with surrendering control to God, and allowing God to His work in us. God takes into consideration the gifts that He has designed us with. When looking at the Proverbs 31 woman, it is not meant to make you feel incompetent, deficient, or intimidated. Look at it as a door from which to see yourself as God sees you, through His eyes.

I recall the words of the co-founding pastor of a church I attended. She was teaching a series of the Proverbs 31 woman to a large group of ladies. I was new to living the life as a believer and was unfamiliar with the Book of Proverbs. She said, "The Proverbs 31 woman is not just that woman over there, or someone who has reached a certain status, or the woman in her older years." She went on to say, "She is you and me. You are, we are, I am, the Proverbs 31 woman." This is not only the woman we aspire to be, but this is who we are. As women, often-times we are quick to compare ourselves to others. We compare our lives from the grand scheme to the most minute detail. As you study the chapter of Proverbs 31, envision reading about yourself. As you study Proverbs 31, seek God's wisdom on areas that require fine-tuning. Allow God to reveal to you on how to become stronger and more competent in certain areas that this chapter speaks to. Proverbs 31 stems from a mindset and identity that comes through your relationship with Christ.

When studying the Proverbs 31 woman, I like to categorize into the following: personal traits, business and professional life, family, and passion work.

When reading about this woman, there is a sense of meek-ness, beauty, wisdom, and strength that she, the Proverbs 31 woman, exudes. The Proverbs 31 woman and you are one and the same, my dear one. So allow me to rephrase. There is a sense of meekness, beauty, wisdom, and strength that you exude. Do you know who you are, dear one? You are God's beloved. You are royalty. You are priesthood. You are the head and not the tail. You are a citizen of heaven. You, my dear one, are created with the most precious hands and purest heart. You, my fellow Proverbs 31 sister, are an advocate for those less fortunate, under-represented, and impoverished. This speaks to the passion work category. *You* are fierce as *you* are a force to be reckoned with. *You* boldly use *your* voice, *your* actions, and *your* life to defend the rights of the voiceless and disadvantaged. Examine your life as to who have been called and positioned to speak on behalf of. Your children, individuals with disabilities, single moms, teen moms, seniors and the aged? Similar to Deborah in the Book of Judges, as she was a wise woman who others sought guidance, advice, and direction from because she was just and spoke to righteousness.

As we move further through the Book of Proverbs chapter 31, it begins to speak to what is referred to as noble character for a wife. This section falls into the family category. Let us, as women, not only see this as it relates to being a wife and traits considered desirable in a wife, but the identity God has called us to evolve into, whether married or single. As a Proverbs 31 woman, *you* are worthy and invaluable to your loved ones. *You* are trustworthy, competent, a vessel of God's light, being of encouragement, and are a woman of great influence. *You* will go to the ends of the earth to be a positive influence to *your* loved ones, including husband, children, and close people in *your* life to make them feel comfortable, comforted, secure, and provided for. *Your* presence and intentionality brings good and abundance to *your* family. *You* ensure that the needs of *your* family are priority because you understand that *your* home is *your* first ministry as *your* home does not go without, for *your* family is fed, clothed, has shelter, and the bills are tended to. More than the physical needs, but *you* ensure that the emotional and spiritual needs of your household are tended to. Your children and legacy call you blessed as they watch your life boldly unfold as *you* walk in *your* purpose.

Studying the chapter gives a picture of how the Proverbs 31 woman is a business-minded individual describing a work ethic that is appreciated by women in the corporate world and the entrepreneur alike. As a woman with this work ethic, it is vital to remember to use what God has placed in *your* hands. Do not be afraid to use the talents, giftings, and the unique way that God has created you. And when there is fear, still pushing past the fear and having the courage to move out of your comfort zone. *You* have a keen eye as *you* pay attention to detail. *You* are resourceful. *You* know your financial affairs, as in, *you* are aware of your daily, weekly, monthly, annual, five year, and long-term income and expenses. *You* are always on the lookout for new opportunities for growth and income options. *You* select *your* projects with love and care. Proverbs 31 speaks to a woman who wakes up early, falls asleep late, and does not lead an idle or unproductive life-style. I know what you are thinking. Does this woman ever sleep? Feeling pressured and overwhelmed just studying the Proverbs 31 woman. Be aware of the unspoken. Because Proverbs 31 speaks to a woman, who, with a strong work ethic, we can extract the following: she has implemented a home of structure where her home is her first ministry, she has determined priorities and necessities versus less important items, and she has built a net-work of support with her husband, children, and those who are named her "female servants," who assist with the caring of chil-dren and tending to the home. This allowed her to tend to her duties while engaging in her own overall well-being.

Throughout the text, the traits of the Proverbs 31 woman is interwoven into the heart of the chapter. Remember, the Proverbs 31 woman is you, beloved. *You* are a woman of integrity, wise, and you always have a word of godly instruction. *You* hold a position of honor and respect. *You* are beautiful and captivating.

Practical Application

This chapter is littered with practical information. It is exploring the ability to recognize the signs of the Superwoman mindset. This may occur in stages, and may not be revealed in one setting, as it requires introspection and prayer time with our Heavenly Father. Let us begin with your heart. Yes, the most difficult, but yet this is where the transformation begins. When you understand the heart of God, you will allow His work to be done in all areas of your life. As you read about the Superwoman syndrome, the women in survival mode, and the overcompensater, what thoughts popped up? What emotions were evoked? How does your heart respond to the symptoms of each? Our lives are a journey with endless opportunities for growth, so let us be vulnerable to what God has to share. When speaking of physical and emotional manifestations of the Superwoman, overcompensater, or the one in survival mode, be open to changing your paradigm and see the Proverbs 31 woman in you.

Identify observations of what you have observed within and of yourself, or observations as shared from the perspectives of others. The heart, the mind, and the behaviors that are manifested must be addressed. Have you noticed how your feelings or thoughts may change regarding certain situations or tasks? Take inventory of all the various roles that you play, and the many groups, situations, activities, and tasks that you are involved in. What are your emotions before, during, and after activities and tasks? Are there patterns that you have noticed?

When exploring your heart, what is the source of engaging in this type of mindset? What experiences do you feel led or contribute to this way of thinking and functioning? Perhaps you do not see a link. Explore this more in your prayer time for God to reveal. This is not a task that I would suggest you do alone if you have past or history of trauma or Adverse Childhood Experiences (ACEs). These are traumatic events occurring before the age of 18, and may include divorce, DV, abuse, incarceration, death (and more), and how these experiences negatively impact the child as adults. In *Preventing Adverse Childhood Experiences (ACEs): Leveraging the Best Available Evidence*, Centers for Disease Control and Prevention (2019) assert that with early detection, early intervention, and implementing interventions, once it has been screened, are crucial. It is strongly recommended that if this is the situation, please begin to address and move through this process with the right clinical therapist for you, meaning, someone who is clinically and educationally trained and clinically licensed to help you.

Identify your needs and write them clearly and simply. Oftentimes, women are socialized and cultivated to see this exercise as selfish and self-absorbed. God created us, all of His children, to be in connection with one another. We were not created to do life alone nor to function as a separate entity. We are to collaborate with, partner with, and help each other be our best selves and live our best God-destined lives. Divide your needs into physical needs and social needs. Do you feel that the areas that you need help pertain to tangible items such as resources as public health benefits and cash aid or childcare, transportation? Are your needs more so emotional such as a need for clinical therapy, spiritual counseling, or support group? Or perhaps needing someone to be present to offer encouragement and a listening ear as you brainstorm ideas and develop solutions.

Identify and write down if you have a support system or circle of support. Who does that circle consist of? Are they in different arenas, such as within the church setting or your child's school, someone within your neighborhood, or perhaps at work? What is your relationship with each person in your circle? Is it a healthy relationship rooted in God and one of love, trust, respect, compassion, and value to both parties? Is this relationship reciprocal, where both parties bless each other and are present for each other? Your circle of influence should build you up, not tear you down.

As this chapter comes to a close, it is a great opportunity to explore your views, attitude, thoughts, and behaviors. Remember that life is not meant to be done alone. Identify who you have in your support system to assist during the challenging times and be a praise partner during the joys of life. And if you do not have a support system, it is time to develop one. For some of you reading this chapter, you may have identified with the approach of "I don't need help," "I got this," or possibly, "everyone who I allowed into my heart and my circle hurt me." Sweet one, it is time to forgive. Forgiveness is not for them, it is for you. Forgiveness is for your peace, your sanity, and your emotional well-being. Yes, guard your heart cautiously, but do not become a prisoner to it. It was not intended for that. Surrender, allow yourself to be vulnerable to God, be receptive to the direction He is calling you to, and let go so that God can come in, beloved. Allow Him to heal the brokenness so that you may learn to trust again. You will learn to trust others, trust yourself, and most importantly, trust God. When you allow God to bring the walls of pain down, your mindset will begin to change, and you will realize that there are people in this world who truly care for you, love you, and wish the best for you. The following Scripture comes to mind, so I pray that you meditate on it before going into prayer and delving into another big topic for many single women of faith: dating and courtship.

Applicable Scriptures

"Jesus says, 'Come to me, all you who are weary and burdened, and I will give you rest" (Matthew 11:28).

Prayer

My petition to You, Father, is for my dear sister to come to a place of vulnerability. This is not an easy stage to come to, but one that is needed to continue to evolve and grow in their relationship with You, Father. May You reveal the issues of the heart and place Your warriors to support Your beloved daughter.

May these supporters be in the shape of counselors, clinicians, coworkers, neighbors, family via genetics or associations. Help Your daughters as they surrender and allow You to reveal and remove, or purge unhealthy mindsets that are hindering them from being the best mothers, women, and daughters of the Kingdom that You have destined and designed them to be. May they be open to what You have to show them and teach them. Remove all barriers so that they may rise to the women You have called and equipped them to become. Amen.

Chapter 7

To Date or Not to Date, to Court or Not to Court

"Do not be yoked together with unbelievers. For what do righteousness and wickedness have in common? Or what fellowship can light have with darkness?" (2 Corinthians 6:14)

OKAY, LADIES, HERE'S THE CHAPTER THAT some of you may have been waiting for or have possibly purchased the book for. How can we have a conversation about co-parenting with Christ without discussing relationships in our lives? Some may ask why dating and courtship should be a conversation for a book discussing co-parenting. I suppose the question should be: Why not? Dating and courtship is a healthy part for adults, especially parenting adults. Some prefer to wait until the kids are adults while others attempt to date while raising healthy, functional children. While others, both within the secular and non-secular realm, assume that single parents should not have feelings or desires of social and romantic relationships. As a single parent, if you feel that God has led you to not pursue a romantic relationship at the moment, then continue to follow God's lead. If as a single parent, God has opened an opportunity for you to have a romantic life and you follow God's guidance, instruction, and boundaries, then that is good as well. As we move through this chapter, you will come to understand the importance of listening to the voice of God and how His voice plays a role in your love life. And listening to the voice of God is a vital step to achieving harmony in our lives.

For some, they have done the necessary work to move into this season of manifestation. For others, this is a challenging area because it requires you to review your past, identify patterns of unhealthy behaviors and thoughts, identify your preferences and desires, and alignment with God's preferences and desires for you, and to go on a journey of inner healing, restoration, and faith. This may involve addressing unfinished business or remnants that you may be aware of or subconsciously unaware of with previous relationships. It may involve your perception or having a distorted view of reality. Dating and courting can be simplified into the dos and don'ts, but I strive to take this conversation deeper by defining these terms, exploring patterns, such as how to move forward and transition from a season of singleness, and readiness to enter into the chapter of marriage. We will discuss terms that are within this spectrum, including one-night stands, friends with benefits, situationships, cohabitation, and sharing a household with an individual who you may be legally separated from or divorced by.

Dating

The term *dating* is a term that is oftentimes synonymous with courting, with dating being applicable in the secular realm and courtship within the non-secular or faith-based realm. This is not to say that dating will not lead to marriage or that courtship will lead to marriage. As I researched the difference between the two terms and explored the stages of the dating relationship and the stages of the courtship relationship, it was difficult to locate evidenced-based material. Similar to courtship, the early stages of the dating relationship is similar to the job-interviewing process.

It is used as an opportunity to get better acquainted. This is very different from the intent, or lack thereof, in a one-night stand, friends with benefits, and situationship. According to one model of dating stages, individuals enter this opportunity through an attraction, may it be physical or perhaps an emotional attraction, with the presence of the other person bringing pleasant memories or how the individual makes the other feel. Oftentimes, the early stages are known as the honeymoon phase because during this time, each person portrays their best and ideal self. The first stage transitions into the second stage as both individuals become better acquainted. This is the decision-making phase when both parties decide whether to remain as friends only, to sever ties, or to move towards a level of mutual commitment. In the third stage of commitment, both parties have come to a mutual place of exclusivity and monogamy or whichever mutually accepted arrangement. As you leave the commitment and enter the true intimacy stage, the honeymoon phase of the relationship ceases and one's true character is revealed, hopefully. This includes the strengths, areas of improvements, and more. This stage is another point of decision-making of whether to move into the fifth and final stage of marriage proposal.

Another model of the dating process according to McGraw-Hill (2008) describes the first stage as attraction as with the former model. The models differ in the subsequent stages, with the second stage being rituals when shared experiences deepen a bond, such as going to church together or sharing meaningful parts of the other person with each other. This stage is followed by the Information Sharing stage during which the person discloses more personal information, as well as engaging in physical contact. The third stage is characterized by Activities. It is during this stage when the couple engages in activities that allow the two to get to know each other by not only asking the harder questions and requiring more observation, but beginning to open and reveal who they genuinely are in a healthy functional relationship. It is during this stage when personal interests allow mutual acceptance. The Emotional Intimacy stage occurs when a feeling of knowing and being known is experienced. The final stage is the Commitment stage, when both parties feel an attachment and desire to be in a more intimate relationship.

One-Night Stands, Friends with Benefits, Situationships, and Cohabiting.

Other arrangements of this era include one-night stands, friends with benefits, situationships, cohabitation, and sharing a residence between a divorced, legally separated, or never married but once romantically involved couple. A situationship, a relatively new term, involves being involved with someone and not placing a label on this encounter, no matter the length of time. Oftentimes, it involves a sexual relationship and resembles a relationship with an emotional component. A one-night stand involves two individuals who are not in a committed relationship and who have not known each other long mutually decide to engage in a short-term sexual act. In most cases, the two individuals have known each other hours into days or usually no more than a week, and the two do not communicate after their one-night affair, essentially no strings attached unless it results in a lifetime commitment of bringing a child into the world. But what the non-secular world will not share with you is that, although in most cases, one-night stands, and in some cases, situationships, do not end with only physical strings, it always leave spiritual strings or attachments and soul ties. When you are physically intimate with someone, we, as women, and as people in general, may say that we can have sex with someone and not develop an attachment as though we can turn those emotions off, such as turning off a light switch. God created us to be in connection with one another. A commitment between husband and wife, as emphasized in the Bible, is the most sacred covenant between two people in the earthly realm. Why, you may ask? Consider why God emphasizes the importance and necessity for sexual intimacy to occur between husband and wife. Because the act, the art, the gift of sexual intimacy and connection brings two people together, not only physically, but emotionally, and especially, spiritually. It is the gift of becoming one. Have you witnessed the infamous meme on social media where a person is lying in bed with a partner who resembles a demon, a zombie, or something similar, indicating that the "human" is sleeping with someone who is spiritually dead. Despite how one may feel when you are sexually intimate, a transference occurs of spiritual strongholds. This ties into why the Bible speaks of avoiding and escaping from the temptation of fornication. This opens the importance of genuinely getting to know and understand one another, get to know your preferences, what you are willing to entertain or live with versus what are definite "nos." Would the person you are involved with and sexually intimate with be someone whose legacy you would want to be left behind for your children or someone you would want to speak into the lives of your children if you are a single parent?

Courtship

This leads us to courting. As with the dating process, several models of the courtship process exists. One such model is the model proposed by Schnarr, Ferrell, Mae, and Schacht (2013) as she describes five distinct phases for a courting couple, beginning with the Pre-Courtship stage. During this stage, much of the information gathering occurs between the two parties. Most, if not all, interaction is within group settings. Emotional attachment and display are kept minimal. Public and private displays of affection are discouraged and does not occur, especially when there is no commitment between the two individuals. In the following stage, Full-Courtship, some alone time may be permissible and appropriate. No commitment or public or private displays of affection is appropriate. Some emotional attachment may begin to develop in this stage. The Committed Relationship stage soon follows when spiritual counseling is sought as a commitment is mutually understood and future engagement is assumed. Minimal public displays of affection, such as handholding and hugging, may be observed. Stage four, the Engagement phase, not only symbolizes commitment to each other, but commitment to marriage. Pre-marital counseling is oftentimes sought during this stage. Many couples will make their status known to more than friends and immediate family. They will, oftentimes, make a public declaration of their love in stage four. Stage five is the entering of marriage symbolized by the wedding and exchanging of sacred vows in the presence of the officiant, and most importantly, God.

Courtship is dating with purpose. It is dating with godly purpose. It is dating with a God marriage as the desire and goal. There may be some variety on what occurs in each stage, the number of stages, and who is involved in the courtship process. It may involve only the two individuals, with God guiding the two individuals. The process may involve the presence and accountability of parents, an older mentoring couple, church family, and pastoral staff, friends, or married friends. Age and culture may play a role in this process. For younger individuals who may reside with their parents, they may seek parental guidance and accountability in the courtship process compared to a couple in their 30s or 40s, as older individuals may seek the guidance of their pastor or a mentoring married couple. In courtship, the premise is to maintain purity and glorify and honor God with your obedience, self-discipline, and self-control. Each determines appropriate guidelines for themselves within the godly principles and boundaries set forth by the Bible.

As we enter this season of dating, courtship, and marriage, it is vital to have a solid foundation in Christ, beginning with developing your identity in Christ. What contributes to the development of your spiritual identity? It involves having a relationship with God as mentioned and discussed throughout this book. In spending time, true quality time with God, and in prayer and conversation with Him, God will show you how to recognize His voice, how to listen to Him, and how to be obedient through allowing yourself to surrender and be vulnerable with God. I believe that God speaks to us every day through His Word, through subtle whispers in our hearts, through the spiritual guidance of others, through prophesy, through prophetic dreams and visions, and through God-filled sermons. It is influenced by your spiritual ear and how well you are spiritually in-tune with God. And this process may take time as you develop your spiritual ear through practice and faith. You must also develop the ability to discern who is speaking; asking and understanding if the voice is God, the enemy, or your own voice.

When I first gave my life to Christ in 2010, I recall reading a faith-based book. During that time, I would spend hours reading books that were faith-based and written by well-known non-secular authors. One day I was reading one of these books, one on goals and discovering my God-given purpose, and I heard, "Put that book down" in my spirit. I looked up, not in fear and not feeling alarmed, but in wonder. This was the first time that I heard the voice of God in my spirit. I instantly knew that it was a reminder not to become engrossed in reading books, other material, or engaging in other tasks, and not spending time with God and studying His Word. Not to say that reading other literature is not important, beneficial, or informative, but it should never take the place of your relationship and time with God. I absolutely love to read, and continue to make time weekly to do so, and I must remain cognizant that my reading and other tasks do not replace or take priority over God. As time progressed, this muscle of recognizing God's voice strengthened and deepened. Hearing the voice of God was vital in every realm of my life and my love life was no different. God spoke to me in every relationship, interaction, and situationship, but it was a matter of listening and being obedient once the call of instruction was set forth.

Void Fillers

In my own life, I noticed that in my most challenging moments, in the natural realm, I would choose to allow my body to respond in one of two ways: through food or through seeking relationships and sex. Can we speak openly? Why was this the case? Because I somehow felt that I could subconsciously exude some level of control in an area in my life when I felt a lack of control over my life, overall. I sought control and what I thought was comfort, in my own attempt to fill the void and emptiness that only God could fill. This pattern continued over many years. In my last year of doctoral studies, four suitors entered my life, two were new, one was a man I was previously romantically involved with, and another had shared his interest in recent years and wanted to explore this option again. I had not been in an exclusive dating relationship for many years. I had a desire for marriage and to be in a fulfilling healthy marriage, but as it had not happened at that point, I chose to focus on my son, my education, and my career. I chose to buckle down on the last leg of my doctoral dissertation, finalizing my literature review, submitting the original and revisions to the Institutional Review Board for pre-approval of my study, conducting the study, analyzing the data, and interpreting the findings. The son of longtime family friends of my parents and grandparents reached out to me, and after several attempts, I had accepted and responded. We conversed over several months before that ended abruptly. In the midst, a former romantic interest began connecting with me, asking me out to dinner and the such. After several mini-serious conversations on the purpose of reconnecting, we had different views on what we were looking for in each other and whether a future with each other was a goal. And as each suitor would reach out to me, the life of the friendship or prospect of a relationship would fizzle, leaving me puzzled and feeling rejected. So one day during my prayer time with my Heavenly Father, I inquired what the issue was; was I meant to live a life of singleness or was it a matter of timing? God began showing the dynamics of each situation with the four suitors, as well as all the individuals I had been romantically involved with in my past. A pattern was revealed to me in how each entered my life, the dynamics of the relationship, and the way in which each ended. Through conversation, prayer, and revelation, God whispered in my spirit the word, "distractions." Imagine my surprise. "How, Lord, please tell me more? What does that mean?" God proceeded to whisper in my spirit, "They are distractions at this time. I need you to focus on where I am taking you and the legacy that is being prepared through you." It began to unfold and make sense to me that God is not closing the door to relationships, love, companionship and partnership, and marriage. At that time in my life, God began showing me that whenever I felt that I was losing control or I was going through a challenging time, I would seek the male companionship to not only validate who I thought I was, but as a coping mechanism to persevere. It was a distraction because as I started to lose focus on God and focus on the gentlemen, my studies began to suffer. Providing sufficient quality time with my son and family was impacted. When you keep God your focus, all areas of your life fall into alignment with dedication, obedience, and self-control. When you do the natural part, God joins you with the supernatural and extraordinary. Join me as I share a time with you when the Holy Spirit whispered in my spirit.

When the Holy Spirit Speaks

In an earlier chapter, I made reference to distraction from your purpose and distraction from persevering through the journey set before you. There was a time when I noticed whenever my breakthrough was near, I was entering a new season, or coming upon a major accomplishment, I was suddenly hit with a wave of suitors. And the most recent was like no other. You would think that I would have learnt the lesson. Years ago, I met a man through a mutual acquaintance. He was heavily involved in ministry at his church, dressed nice, had a challenging adult past, yet appeared to be transitioning into a better life. There were red flags as my parents were not fond of him, and close friends were not pleased with his behavior and demeanor that appeared controlling, manipulative, and verbally aggressive. This was my first relationship after giving my life to Christ, and had assumed that a man who was heavily involved in church, knew and studied the Word consistently, and appeared to be solid in Christ was the right choice for myself and my son. The Bible was used as a guide to keep me aligned to how he felt I should conduct myself, including whether and when I should voice my concerns and opinions on various topics. I did not have a reference point and had not brought the relationship to God prior to my becoming romantically involved with him. We were sexually intimate, or in other words, fornicating. I knew our fornication was against God's principles and would rationalize by saying that we were going to marry. As time went on, we began to talk about marriage more and decided to go to pre-marital counseling. Soon, it appeared that true intentions became sur-faced, and I ceased the relationship.

He reached out to me the following year and had promised that he had changed his ways, was self-sustaining, and no longer conducted himself in a domineering manner. Again, I had not prayed about returning to the relationship, but my flesh thought that perhaps it was a sincere rekindle, we would marry, and all would be well. Parts of his character began to unravel within the first month of becoming recommitted to each other. Not a healthy mindset for me to have. I knew something was wrong. In the world, one refers to it as our gut, intuition, and instinct. In the body of Christ, we know this as the Holy Spirit. As he brought up the idea of marriage, I became more confused. He would visit our home every weekend after work. On this particular Friday, he called, stating that he was exhausted and would not visit that day. I went into prayer with a sincere heart, repenting for not entering this relationship a second time in God's way, in God's timing, and without God's permission. I reminded the Holy Spirit, as though He needed reminding, that we were discussing marriage again. I told the Holy Spirit that I knew something was wrong and I did not want to expose my son nor myself to a sit-uation that was emotionally unhealthy and spiritually unsound. I requested God to reveal to me his true intentions, and not only should marriage be of conversation, but whether this was the man whom God had called to be my husband and to be a father figure to my son. I ended my time with God that Friday night. The following day, my boyfriend called again and said that he was busy and would not visit that day. He agreed to visit Sunday. Again, I knew something was off, as this was not a regular prac-tice. I trusted the Lord and His plan. On Sunday, I had not heard from him and my flesh became impatient. It was 10:30 that night, and my phone notification beeped. As I picked up my phone, I saw his name flash on my text message notification. Excitedly,

I opened the message, and although it was sent to me, it was intended for another woman whom he was wooing. I instantly responded, informing him that I was not the same woman who the text was intended. I know, a regular soap opera. Allowing himself time to deliberate, he reached out an hour later with a story as an attempt to cover. Hurt and in tears, I did not understand why this was happening. He shared that his mother was in the hospital, and him wooing another woman was involving his mother in the hospital.

I awoke early the next day, purchased a bouquet of flowers, and visited his mother before going to work, as I knew this was to be my last time seeing her because I realized that this relationship was not in God's divine plan. I recall sitting on the side of his mother's hospital bed while we talked for an hour. He called his mother while I was there, appearing shocked that I was there in his absence. His mother made a statement that stayed with me. She said, "Chanel, I don't think my son likes me." I did not understand and assumed that perhaps she was experiencing the side effects of medication. I smiled and offered a general response, "Oh no, your son loves you," as I looked into her eyes. She replied, "I know that he loves me, but I don't think he likes me." I sat there with a smile on my face, in silence, and a broken heart asking myself whether I want to pursue a relationship, friendship, or any other association with a person whose mother did not feel cared for, protected, and respected by him. My response was no, and as I hugged her, prayed with her, and said our goodbyes, I knew that was my last time seeing her. Unbeknownst to me at the time, that although the evening before was the physical demise of our relationship, this was the continuation of pain that stemmed in rejection, insecurity, the beginning of bitterness, resentment, and fear of meeting and dating men who claimed to have a personal relationship with God. In other words, I developed a fear of dating men who claimed to be not only Christian, but born-again believers, serving, living, and breathing Christ.

This was my first relationship after giving my life to Christ, and my unhealthy thought was that abuse and abusive behavior from your partner, and abusive dynamics was a normal part of a healthy relationship, especially a healthy relationship with a "believing" man. And over time and healing, God began a work in me of identifying irrational thought patterns and beliefs; thus, changing how I would perceive romantic relationships and partners.

Weeks later, while in my prayer closet, I realized that God answered my prayer as the Holy Spirit confirmed what He had already revealed during the red flags. I was amazed at how quickly and succinctly God answered my prayer and spoke to me. This story of my personal experience is not to speak poorly of men who identify as Christian believers, but it is a testament to hear the voice of God in every area of your life, including your love life. This brings us to my love journey.

My Love Journey

My love journey consciously began in December 2010. I was a woman with promiscuous behaviors from the age of 18 through my early 30s, with a scatter of one-night stands, to friends with benefits, to situationships, and long-term relationships, all for the sake of searching for love, filling the void, and becoming validated. Yes, filling a void that only God could fill, filling a void that only God's love could and would fill if I allowed Him to.

I gave my life to Christ, became born-again on July 27, 2018, one day after my birthday. I was in a sexually intimate relationship with someone I was not married to. I went out to celebrate with my friends and family. Early the following day, my boyfriend arrived to my home in his Sunday best. I was taken aback as I had smeared eye make-up and a tank top. We were intimate. I remember sitting there on the bed with a blanket over me, watching him put his suit on. I asked where he was going, and he responded by sharing that he was going to church to give glory to God. I recall asking him, "Do you feel weird? We just slept together. Do you feel ashamed?" And he responded no because God knew his heart. I responded to my own shame and guilt. I fell asleep shortly after he left. I had this dream that was the first of a lifetime of prophetic dreams from the Lord. There was a man in my dream with a ring of fire surrounding us. This man with rage in his eyes was holding me up by my shirt, and I began pleading the blood of Jesus. Although I had not talked to God in such a long time, it was as though my spirit knew what to do and how to respond. As I awoke, my lips continued to move, my voice continued to whisper, and my spirit cried the blood of Jesus over my life. As I drove to my parents' house later that day to pick up my son, I knew that I needed to call my dear friend. Our conversation went like this: "Sis, I don't know what kind of dream that was (after I explained in detail), but I feel like God is telling me that it's time to come home. Like it's time to get my life right and give it over to Him." My friend chuckled and responded in a way that I knew she had a smile on her face, "I think it's time for you to come to church with me." The following Sunday, my son and I went to her church, where we remain twelve years later. The following week I told my boyfriend that I could no longer sleep with him because God had something better in store. I did not know what that was at the time, but it was God's best in abundance. One month later, I responded to the altar call and gave my life to God, and my then young son soon did the same in children's ministry.

Fast forward to the date mentioned, December 2010. My son and I had moved into our first home on September 30th of that year where I closed escrow just one week before. On this particular date, my son and I had arrived home from a lovely train ride with other parents and children. My son was content with watching cartoons in the living room while I had commune time with God. It had been two years since I gave my life to Christ at this point and had begun my celibate lifestyle. I knew that God had some words to share, so I grabbed my Bible, pen, and journal and laid on my bed, which led to a six-hour conversation of me listening, studying, and writing. I shared my heart with God. As Psalm 37:4 states, "Delight yourself in the Lord and He will grant you the desires of your heart." So there I was pleading my case to God as to why I did not want to live a life of singleness. God answered so clearly by whispering in my spirit, "Before I can take you to that next season of marriage, I need to show you how to love before I reveal to you who I have for you to love." God took me on a study throughout the Bible on love. As He showed me the different types of love, what that looked like, how that was manifested, and how to move in His love, I remained in awe of this process. As my Bible study and time with God came to an end that evening, I went into prayer followed by my silence. God whispered in my spirit, "Your husband is coming." I cried tears of joy, tears of pain, tears of fear, every emotion you could think of because I knew that was the beginning of a journey. Unbeknownst to me of how long the journey was going to be. And throughout the years, in my most difficult times, in my moments of doubt, in my moments of rejection, in my moments of healing, in moments when my faith was tested, in moments of conviction, guilt, shame, and "Darn it, I messed up again" mindset, I found myself holding onto that Word, holding onto that promise.

So this leads me to inquire about your relationship with Christ. Yes, your relationship with God is the underlying tone for this book project of love, but it is a vital key to this chapter. This chapter is dedicated to our single ladies, our single moms.

A word to the wise. For those of you who are currently separated, legally or by circumstance (have not submitted the forms or started the process), I would strongly encourage you not to seek a romantic relationship until you are legally separated and recommended until your divorce is finalized. Additionally, I encourage you to be in spiritual and or clinical counseling and guidance to identify the reasons for this status and to identify any underlying unresolved feelings, situations, or thought processes before you move forward with another relationship.

I began this section with my personal story of how I came to give my life to Christ. Why, you may ask? Your relationship with God, your identity in Christ, and your vulnerability to recognize and hear the voice of God, and act on His word, and take His lead is the root of how you interact with others, may it be relationships with family, platonic relationships, associations, and romantic relationships. How does God communicate with you? Are you able to recognize the voice of God? What does that look like? I ask these questions because when you are receptive, the Holy Spirit will guide you and teach you through your love journey as with all facets of life. The Holy Spirit is purposed to protect you, to guard you, and to bring clarity and understanding. This leads me to the act of submission. What is that noise that I hear? The screeching scream that you yelled, the sigh that you may have unknowingly breathed, the roll of the eye, or the side-eye that you just gave towards this book. Yes, I heard that and felt that.

In all sincerity and seriousness, submission is a beautiful concept when understood in the context that God intended. It is an act of service, of compassion, and of love. I am not necessarily speaking about submission in the context of marriage or in a relationship to your husband only, but within the context of your relationship with God. Submission is not to demean, belittle, disrespect, or to put or keep a woman in a subservient position. Submission is meekness in its most pure state. It is to yield in and within love. In the following Scripture:

"Submitting to one another out of reverence for Christ. Wives, submit to your own husbands, as to the Lord. For the husband is the head of the wife even as Christ is the head of the church, his body, and is Himself its Savior. Now as the church submits to Christ, so also wives should submit in everything to their husbands" (Ephesians 5:21-24).

Meekness is knowing and recognizing the Holy Spirit and being obedient to how the Holy Spirit guides you. It is knowing when to be silent. It is knowing when, if, and how to speak. Because not every thought needs to be said. Or it may not need to be said at that time. Nor said in how your flesh wants to deliver it.

I am reminded of a time when I had a conversation with a superior through a previous employer. I had recently graduated with my master of arts degree and had a desire to promote. At the time, I naively assumed that everyone who is in my life, may it be professional, family members, or others had my best interest at heart. A sister in Christ had shared through conversations to be mindful of my interaction with this individual. I took this advice with a grain of salt and assumed that perhaps she was mistaken of this individual's true intentions as this individual would share stories of her being a single mother and how she persevered, so I mistook her for more of an ally than an adversary. I walked into my superior's office and requested to speak with her. She graciously complied and asked me to sit down. I shared that I wanted to apply for the senior counseling position. She smiled and enthusiastically shared that she agreed that this was the next logical step. She offered to assist me with my application and write a letter of recommendation. With this in mind, I quickly applied. Approximately three weeks later, I requested to speak with her again. She complied and sat across from me at her desk with a serious, almost annoyed facial expression. I shared that I had applied for the position, had yet to receive contact, and sought guidance from her on how I should proceed. Her response caught me off guard as she quickly recanted her statements from weeks before, sharing that the position was a better fit for another young woman who I started the agency with years before. Furthermore, she had helped the other young lady secure the position by helping her with her application, possible mock interview, and offered references for her. Her approach was matter-of-fact, and she ended with a subtle yet awkward stare, waiting for my reaction. Stunned, I sat there, questioning in my mind what I *thought* I heard only a few short weeks prior to that moment. I do not have a confrontational demeanor, yet I remember having a flood of emotions rising up in the flesh, from anger, rejection, pain, humiliation, embarrassment, to invalidated feelings. My flesh wanted to react by questioning her, yet the Holy Spirit stepped in, and wisdom and discernment took over at the moment, calling me to respond and not react. I sat there patiently, with legs crossed at the ankles, a smile on my face, and an attempt at having joy in my heart, as I knew that questioning her or showing even the slightest of emotion would be misconstrued as aggression or hostility. The Holy Spirit instructed me not to react, but to respond in silence. But you ask how? It was an act of God. As I walked out of her office, holding back tears because of being upset, God began to use that moment as a teachable moment for growth. God began to reveal what areas I was wrong, areas that required growth and improvement, and how to proceed. God will use moments such as this to reveal the character of others, reveal your heart, and most importantly, reveal the true amazingly beautiful character of God, the ultimate teacher and counselor.

This personal story demonstrates that the Holy Spirit reveals that not every word needs to be said, that not every thought needs to be spoken aloud, that not every emotion needs to be acted upon or shown on one's face, and that silence is just as powerful as words when commanded by the Holy Spirit. This is meekness as it uses the wisdom and discernment of God to know when to speak, when to be silent, and when God instructs you to speak, understanding that delivery and the timing of that message is crucial. Developing a meek character is not only helpful in your professional life, but is absolutely vital in your personal life, especially with regards to your romantic relationships and within the context of marriage.

God's Timing versus Our Own

How did your flesh respond when you read the subtitle? Have you heard of the saying that God is always on time? It may not be when *we* feel that God is needed or when *we* believe that God should intervene in a particular situation. At some point, hopefully, we realize that there are some factors that remain out of our human control, and time is one of them. No matter what we do, how we choose to spend our time, the one understood reality is that we all have the same twenty-four-hour period of time. At times, we may believe that we can somehow manipulate time, but I have a little secret-come closer. Come a tad bit closer-WE CANNOT! Understanding this truth is the first part of understanding that things, situations, changes, and seasons occur when God feels that we are ready, not ready according to ourselves, not ready according to others, but ready according to Him.

As Ecclesiastes emphasizes,

"To everything there is a season, and a time to every purpose under the heaven: A time to be born, and a time to die; a time to plant, and a time to pluck up that which is planted; A time to kill, and a time to heal; a time to break down, and a time to build up; A time to weep, and a time to laugh; a time to mourn, and a time to dance; A time to cast away stones, and a time to gather stones together; a time to embrace, and a time to refrain from embracing; A time to get, and a time to lose; a time to keep, and a time to cast away; A time to rend, and a time to sew; a time to keep silence, and a time to speak; A time to love, and a time to hate; a time of war, and a time of peace" (Ecclesiastes 3:1-8).

Our lives occur in seasons. Explore and identify the season that God has you in currently. Are you in a season of waiting? Are you in a season of working in His assignment? Perhaps it is a season of transition? It is important to be in communication with God and allow Him to guide you on how to move through this season so that we are not out of order. Sometimes we have the tendency to move and create what I called the man-made blessing. It is what we disguise as something we see as a blessing, but out of alignment with God's will, either due to God having something better in store for us or us making a conscious decision to move in our own timing and not God's because of our impatience. And then we hope that God blesses our disobedience or repairs what we chose to do. God blesses us with free will, and He will allow us to live out the consequences of actions that we chose if that is what God has chosen for us.

As we speak of seasons and God's timing in our lives, I am reminded of several night dreams that God had given in which He whispered words of encouragement to continue to trust Him along my love journey. I am reminded of three dreams that I had in recent years Along my love journey, I had moments of uncertainty, loneliness, and questions, as can be expected at times. It was during these times when I leaned on God, sought wisdom from my circle of influence, and chose to allow God to lead me on my faith walk. The first dream was a time when I was seeking God for direction regarding a romantic companion.

When God Speaks through dreams
He Is Coming

One fact that is known about me is my love for listening to spiritually-based podcasts, social media videos, courses, programs, and the like. These videos focus on overall well-being, business and entrepreneurship, spiritual guidance and biblical principles, and professional, academic, and personal development. I live a fast-paced lifestyle, so I love to get bites and nuggets of wisdom throughout my day while driving with the audio playing. I listen while at work, during a walk, or during a treadmill jog. Again, ensuring that listening to audio did not take the place of or take precedence over God, but were tools. These items were tools that I used on my journey.

One of the well-known ladies I follow is a woman who is a first-generation pastor who pastors with her husband. Her ministry focuses on developing single and married women, the call that God has on their lives, and guiding single Christian women to lead spiritually healthy and sound lives.

One night, I had a dream that I was at her house. Her home was a lavish mansion, overseeing the lit city. It had a spectacular view. She was hosting an elegant, yet intimate dinner party with mostly eligible ladies and bachelors. After dinner, I found myself sitting on this table with tall chairs in the backyard, enjoying the view while skimming through a book. This hosting pastor and another woman, who had not spoken with me prior, walked up to me and said, "He's coming." My response to her was a confident, "Yes, I know," with a smile on my face and a God confidence that this statement was transferring to my real life outside of the dream. What God reminded me in this season was to continue to look to Him, continue to focus on His assignment, and in God's timing will my husband and I be revealed to each other. God has a lovely way of speaking to us.

Our Wedding Day

Another dream occurred years ago, perhaps a couple years after I became a born-again believer, when I was in prayer about my husband. There were times when I felt called to pray for my husband, not necessarily for him to be presented to me, but for me to pray for his well-being, strength, and wisdom to move through a challenging moment or season in his life. In my spirit, I felt that I needed to pray for his future, yet not knowing who he was. I needed to pray for God to guard his heart. I felt a yearning to pray for his ability to navigate through challenging times and for the grace of God to cover him and for him to recognize the voice of God when He speaks. During this season, I dreamt that I was in a white dress with a white hat with small white netting covering my right eye and right side of my face, indicating that I was slightly older because it was a style more commonly perceived to be for a more mature woman. I was standing at the bottom of a staircase with a tall robust man walking towards me. He was dressed in a black tux. As he was walking down the staircase towards me, the view of his body went up to his neck. My view of him would not go above his neck. It was apparent by our attire and the setting that it was our wedding day. It was the two of us as there were no family members or familiar faces among us as though we marrying in a distant place. I believe that this dream was symbolic of several things: unity, intimacy between two beings, and not to be afraid to travel a road less traveled with little familiarity when God is leading you. It was a pivotal moment in my spiritual life.

Preparing Us for Each Other

Recently, God began to minister to my spirit my journey toward marriage. Once again, it was a moment when I asked

God for encouragement and strength to stay on this path of purity and purpose. This was a time when my faith began to lessen, and I knew I needed God to breathe into me, to remind me of what He shared with me many years ago that my husband was coming. On this night, I found myself sitting on my bed, eyes closed, and having a heart-to-heart with Jesus, confessing my doubts, my heart's troubles, and my questions. Once I realized my fears and cast my burdens onto Him and read my Bible, I laid down, hoping for an answered prayer sooner than later.

That night, I dreamt of myself in a large room that resembled a dance studio where ballet dancers would typically practice. It had white walls surrounded by large windows on every wall and a beautiful oakwood floor. The natural sunlight beamed through the windows to the left of us as though it were early morning. I stood there facing east of the sunlight with a beautiful flowy white bridal gown. To the left of me stood my husband dressed in a black tux. In this dream, I was able to see the silhouette and subtle features of his face. We held hands and proceeded to position ourselves to dance. There was no audience, no family members, just us with one important guest, Jesus. Before we could begin our life of slow dancing, Jesus stood in the middle of both us, facing us. And before Jesus released this man to be my husband, Jesus walked up to my husband and began fixing his tie, straightening the shoulders of his tux, and I stood there, not looking at my husband, but had my eyes on Jesus. I understood what God was telling me. My future husband and I are in the preparation season as God is preparing us for one another and for marriage. So for you, my sister, with the desire for marriage, allow God to continue to do a work in you and your future mate. Be patient, be proactive, and diligent in seeking God. Do not lose focus on Him as the foundation of marriage rests upon your preparation season, and this season, my dear one, is not one to rush. As we move through different seasons, it is vital to remain in communication with God, being receptive to His instruction, spiritual confirmation, and moving in His timing and not my own.

You'll Be Found in Ministry

A few weeks ago, I was casually thinking of a question that someone asked me years ago, did I choose career and education over marriage or the opportunity of marriage? Does it have to be a choice? It is the age-old question, can we have it all? Can we really have it all? Is it all? We serve a God who is faithful and wants to grant us our desires, providing that they are aligned with God's plan and His word for our lives. Do we feel that if an event, a goal, a "something" has not happened in our timing and in the way we envisioned, that it will not happen? So I took it to the Lord and began sharing my heart because although we profess the statement of faith and the promises of God, it is another thing to fully live it out and walk it out in our day-to-day as we are presented with distractions and situations that say something different. A few nights later, not thinking back to the conversation that I had with God, I had a dream that I was in a church delegating a task and passing out flyers related to ministry. I was dressed casually, and a man with a baseball cap worn sideways motioned to me that he wanted to talk. I gestured to him to come join me at the table with a smile on my face; he walked over and sat down on the other side of the table facing me. I said, "Hey, how are you?" The position of the hat informed me that he was young, not spiritually or emotionally, but chronologically, in comparison to me. The nature of our conversation let me know that we had known each other for quite some time and were friends. I had known him to be a decent guy and never thought of anything more than an acquaintanceship. He looked at me and confidently began to profess his feelings. I recall being taken aback in the dream. He spoke to how he had known me for a long time, and every time he saw me, he noticed that I was always serving others and working in ministry. He began sharing his love and he said, "You are my song." I woke up with so much joy in my heart as confirmation that I must continue serving in and focus on ministry, God's work, and marriage will come. The veil of singleness will be removed, and the man whom God has called to be my husband will be attracted without me noticing.

What does this mean, you may ask? Or how does this apply to you and your life? Continue to allow God to shape you and fine-tune your purpose. Continue to work, walk, and serve in God's ministry and His purpose for you. For those who desire marriage, a God-destined marriage, allow the gentleman to find you. I know people, especially women, have very strong views on what waiting for marriage looks like. Allow me to remind you, there is a difference between *waiting* and *serving in ministry while preparing*. There are various Scriptures that describe the difference, so let us explore. What are you doing in this season, whether it is marriage or another heart's desire? There is pro-active waiting, and then there is passive waiting, such as in the Scripture, "*Be still and know that I am* God." Waiting denotes a sense of action in inaction. By being still, it is understood that you have done and continue to move as God instructs in the natural, and God will meet you at your heart's desire and need. This is proactive waiting. Have you ever known someone, that one person, who every time they see you, they comment, "Girl, you know I'm looking for a job, are you hiring or know someone?" The one time you decide to take them up on their offer and inquire further with questions such as, "How's your resume?" "Do you have a copy of your CV or resume?" "What type of position are you looking for?" "What is your expertise?" and they look at you with a puzzled expression of, "I have no idea what you are talking about." A job that God has provided for you is not going to come without a level of preparation on your part, may it be the journey you have endured thus far or another situation. As you allow God to prepare you for marriage, be proactive in knowing that God is not preparing you for the wedding, but for the marriage. Be open, vulnerable, receptive, and humble as God reveals areas about yourself that require God's healing, restoration, and redemption. Is it unfinished business? Are there spiritual strongholds? Is there history of trauma? Is there history of abuse in your past during childhood or past relationships? Is there history of divorce with you personally or between your parents? Is there a level of decency and order in your life? I am not saying that your life must be one of perfection, by any means, as *we all fall short of the glory of God*. I am not saying that your life has to be squeaky clean. What I am saying is to allow God to reveal and identify for you areas that may hinder certain aspects of your marriage, such as communication, sexual intimacy, emotional intimacy, issues of the heart, spiritual identity, and spiritual roles.

But for a Season

In November 2017, God began to reveal programs that would benefit single mothers. This led to a God-inspired faith-based male mentorship program. As the Scriptures, program structure, and details began to fall into place, I began asking God for people with expertise in designing mentorship programs geared towards boys and young men, in particular, those of color.

A man I had known for many years through our parents and grandparents had come to mind. The event that brought us together was the death of my grandmother, and we met as young eighteen to twenty year olds. We were fond of each other and had stayed in contact via telephone for a few years. This continued until after I gave birth to my son, and within months, we stopped talking due to a mishap, which he later apologized for. Years later, he reached out to me via social media. I ignored his first attempt. He reached out again a year later, and I again ignored his attempts. On the third attempt, I accepted, and we talked for hours to clear the air of what occurred so many years before. Within months, we spoke of him flying out to see me. I was hesitant because years had passed, and we needed time to become reacquainted as older, more mature adults. I recall the first time he made mention of him visiting me, I instantly went into prayer when we hung up the phone. I recall asking God, "God, you know my heart. You know my heart's desire. If it is not meant for him to come, if the timing is wrong, I pray that the door to this visit be closed." Nothing more was said in prayer. He and I continued to chat on the phone, and as the discussed time frame approached for his visit, he shared that he was unable to visit. I was not upset as I smiled and whispered to God, "Thank you." Was I disappointed? Somewhat, but once again, God answered prayers, and I did not question it as I knew God had His reasons. If it was meant to be, then the door would be once again opened and God would allow it. He then mentioned to visit possibly during the holidays. I was open and immediately upon hanging up, I prayed, "God, I only want to do what is pleasing to You. If his intentions are not pure, if he is not meant to be my husband whom You have for me, or if this is not Your timing, then close this door, not through sickness or the death of someone, but simply close it." I said nothing more in prayer. Time approached, and we spoke as though it was still a possibility for him to visit.

In the midst of our long-distance chats, God placed an idea in my heart about a program that would bless single female-headed households. As I began developing the faith-based male mentorship program, I was reminded that this gentleman had substantial mentoring experience. So one day, I called him up, and we spoke for about two hours of me asking questions and him sharing his wealth of knowledge. It was a beautiful moment, and I will forever be grateful to him for sharing and being an integral part in that season of development in my life. Later that week, I scheduled a meeting to propose my idea to the organization. I had my meeting and it went well. Within weeks of the meeting, it was getting closer to him visiting me. We both were busy and I had noticed that he had not reached out to me to confirm his visit, which was tentatively scheduled within the next couple of days. So I called, and he said that he was not going to make it so close to the holidays. Again, disappointed, but trusting God in the process and God had once again answered prayers by closing that door that God did not want open. Months went by and there had not been any communication between us. I refused to call him. Call it pride. Call it wisdom. I am not sure, but I refused to call. Then, one day, he calls me in the month of February or March, sharing that he wanted to visit. No mention of the inconsistency in communication. So once again, the third time, I prayed what was becoming my "Is this Your will?" prayer. Now, allow me to explain. Some may read this and say that perhaps I am closing the door with my prayer. No, this prayer is one that we as believers should be praying before every decision is made, and especially when it involves an area where you know you are most weak and tempted, before we encounter any situation, and before we move forward in any direction in our life. It is imperative that we seek God's wisdom and request that He close doors that need to be shut and open doors that need to be open, and for these opportunities to happen in His timing and in His method of choosing.

Plans were not finalized, but it appeared that he was trying to make arrangements. One evening during a brief phone conversation, he asked, "I plan on getting a hotel, will you be staying with me in the hotel?" insinuating whether we would be sexually intimate. I was not offended by the question. We had discussions prior about faith, relationship with God, and my choice to live a celibate lifestyle despite how difficult of a lifestyle it was at times. I paused before responding and slowly replied, "No." He spoke quietly and said okay. The phone conversation continued for another few minutes before we hung up, with no indication of what was to come. I never heard from him again. Was I hurt? Yes. Were his intentions pure? No. I cannot analyze his reason for responding the way he chose to. All I could do was evaluate the situation from my perspective. Would I have done anything different? No, I cannot say that I would have.

As the months went by, there were moments where I had thoughts and feelings of being rejected, internalizing how someone chose to behave as though it was my fault. I asked God to reveal the importance of each of my recent situationships and connections over the last couple of years, including this brief, rekindled encounter via long distance. A few days later, I was given a dream. In this dream, I was in my car in a drug-infested and crime-ridden area. My son and I were sitting in the car, and I was approached by several people, including this gentleman suitor, who attempted to visit me three times. It was in the back parking lot of a restaurant that people frequented. It was at night. In this dream, this same gentleman suitor had huge bags that had light emanating from them. I was kind to him as I was aware that I knew him. Although not in the safest environment, I felt that my son and I were safe with him standing outside of our car. He looked at me with the softest eyes and appeared to have good intentions towards my son and me. As I got closer and looked into the bags, he began pouring gold and money on us. It was never-ending abundance. I awoke with this peace, and asked God to reveal the meaning of this dream. God began to reveal that He returned this gentleman suitor temporarily back into my life for a purpose, which was to assist in a season of development meant to bring opportunity and godly prosperity. He was not intended to be a permanent fixture or relationship in my life. God further revealed that this gentleman suitor was symbolic of God as I felt that my son and I were safe in his presence. God was showing me that God will always provide for our every need and in abundance. I found peace in that dream and learned to trust God in the process.

Restoration and Healing

Before we go into a full conversation of practical tools to apply in your everyday life as a single and ready-to-mingle gal, there is one place where we should start, and that is restoration and healing. We mentioned this stage in earlier sections of this chapter and throughout the book. What is your motivation for desiring a relationship? Do you desire or love the idea of being in love, of being loved, of being in a relationship, or perhaps the wedding as opposed to the marriage? Is it bizarre to desire these things, to have these thoughts or feelings? No. But my question is meant to get to the root of that desire. Is it a healthy desire? Is it a fear of being alone? Is it the reality that after examining your past romantic relationships, you have been either in a relationship, situationship, or sexually involved with someone, one after the other, since your teenage years? If you have not allowed yourself to go and sit in this place for a long time, then sister, it is time. It is time to explore and go on this journey with God. Where did we begin the journey in the first chapter? With identity. And how do we establish our identity? How do we allow God to show us, mold us, teach us, shape us into the women of God He has created us to become? We begin in a posture of bowing down, on our knees, face down, or prostrate on the floor with a willing heart, a receptive spirit, and in a vulnerable space to surrender all to the One who created us, the One who knows you like no other.

I had my first sexual encounter when I was 18, and it was a domino effect from that point. I was not a rambunctious child or teen. I was always seeking the approval of my parents, especially my mother and those in authority positions. I attended private school for years until my last year of middle school. I was the student who was the cadet battalion commander in her high school cadet program and AP and honors classes throughout high school, who went to a university fresh out of high school. I was the proper, eloquently spoken child, raised in middle-class suburbia. Why do I paint this picture? To give you an inkling of who I was at that stage in my young life? Because no one would believe the second life that I lived in my early undergrad years while working two jobs. I had numerous partners, at times, brief situationships, long-term relationships, and a variety of the two on this spectrum called dating and wild invincible living. Encounter after encounter, dangerous and risky behavior after the next, left me more emotionally scarred, spiritually depleted, and broken. As I fought to fill this void that only God could fill, subconsciously leaving a piece of me with each person, and creating soul ties with each encounter, I could no longer function, as I did not know what a healthy relationship looked like. And do not be fooled. This behavior did not end when I became pregnant with my son at twenty years of age. If anything, my encounters were relationships that lasted from a few months to years in some cases.

I met some great gentlemen along the way, but brokenness attracts brokenness. It gravitates to others. When great male suitors pursued, I did not know how to respond other than push them away with unrealistic expectations as an attempt to guard my heart. This also was exhibited in my behavior towards them with my reaction being controlling in nature, such as when a man would offer suggestions, oftentimes, they would be confronted with attitude, or my aggressive tone. My curt, disrespectful, and cutting words lashed out like a whip and sliced a man's spirit like a sword. Yet, men with brokenness found their way to me and I welcomed it with open arms because I felt not only needed, but validated. It feels good to be needed right? No, this was dysfunctional and illogical thinking. Subconsciously, my behavior felt that I could save those whose true saving grace was God and having a relationship with Him. What did this look like? It was the propensity of me choosing men and falling in love with men who were emotionally unavailable and men who were not ready or willing to commit to anyone, but specifically to me. Allow that last statement to sit and marinate for a moment. And the more relationships I engaged in that ended with cheating or simply fizzled out, the more I internalized it, the harder my heart became towards relationships, and in the midst, I put up a mask, a façade. I began to question whether God had marriage in mind for me. I began to internally believe the lies that I was not good enough, that I was insufficient, was not worthy, was incomplete without a significant other, and perhaps was not deserving of a "happily ever after." I began to internalize the belief that perhaps it was me, so I would become awkward around men as an attempt to become noticed. I would engage in behavior that was far from modest to get noticed, from the scantily clad clothing to becoming quickly sexually intimate, because if they could see my worth in my body or in my desire to please them over myself, then I would be loved. In my story, it was through my risky behavior through which my pain was manifested. What is yours? Is your void being filled by another type of behavior or addiction? Is it overeating? Is it drugs or an attraction to substances, both legal and illegal? Is it an addictive behavior such as the need to feel that you need to have everything under your control, such as your minor or adult children, your significant other, or those around? And when things are not appearing to be in your control, you lash out in anger or display manipulative or victimized behavior? Yes, completely out of character.

What am I describing here? Sharing these moments of my life is not meant to bring the mood down, but to create a reality check in all of us, a "sister, let's get real, raw, and transparent" moment with you. Do these thoughts, feelings, or behaviors sound painfully familiar, perhaps in your own life or you have observed this behavior in others? You may ask, how does one know if healing is what is needed, and how does one know the area where healing is the tool? Take inventory of your life and your relationships, especially those closest to you. If you feel prayerfully compelled to ask those around you of their assessment of your interaction with them, and if they truly believe that you will not retaliate against them, you may be shocked what they disclose. Explore patterns in your life. Evaluate relationships with your children. How is their behavior towards you? Are people allowed to be themselves when in your presence? Do you have appropriate boundaries in place? Are you a people-pleaser, always seeking the approval of others, always asking permission to be who God has called you to? Are you in a place of genuine growth, always seeking to grow spiritually and grow in knowledge and wisdom? Is there a sense of dissonance in your life? Are there discrepancies and inconsistencies in your life, your thoughts and emotions, from your behaviors? What about this next important indicator: your health? Are you constantly physically ill, stressed, or experiencing burn out? Are you experiencing decision fatigue? A common experience among single mothers when one avoids making decisions, even minor decisions, due to the emotional and sometimes physical stress that comes with that decision or situation.

Genuine healing and restoration come from God and may come in the form of a combination of His Word, wise mentors, clinically trained therapists, spiritual counselors, support groups, and getting into your prayer closet and allowing God to minister to you. I believe that as a society, we focus so heavily on being in a relationship or getting married that we tend to lose focus on being whole and restored. When we are whole and restored, we are in a place to recognize when God has brought someone in our lives instead of us settling for what God had not intended. Sister, I ask you to go on a journey of healing from past hurts, intergenerational transmission, and strongholds that we have either brought into our lives or was placed on us by others. This step of godly healing should be first on your journey to desiring a God-filled equally-yoked courtship and marriage. Once this has taken place, we are in a better position spiritually when placing boundaries because we understand the price that has been paid for us and the life God has called us to live.

Boundaries

This section is comprised of both spiritual and practical application.

"Don't be misled-you cannot mock the justice of God. You will always harvest what you plant...so let's not get tired of doing what is good. At just the right time we will reap a harvest of blessing if we don't give up" (Galatians 6:7,9).

Let us define boundaries. It is a line of demarcation meant to establish limitations, rules, and associated behavior that are both appropriate and inappropriate. I will provide an example. For instance, in the previously mentioned dream, my suitor asked if I had plans to stay in the hotel with him. My flesh desired to say yes, but the Holy Spirit provided an escape from being tempted in the main area that was a temptation: fornication. This was a boundary I set for myself. You may ask why dating must be so formalized, but again, let us remember that we are not intending to casually date, but we are discussing courtship with the intended purpose of marriage. As we discuss boundaries, be mindful that there are general boundaries according to the Bible, there are boundaries, or lack thereof, within the world, and boundaries that you have or should create for yourself based on your personality, your history, emotional and spiritual strongholds, patterns, and areas that you may have had or have tendency to struggle with. While we are on the topic, what are your personal boundaries? Do you have boundaries? What are your standards as it pertains to dating, courtship, or any relationships and friendships, generally speaking in your life may it be professional, business, ministry and church related, and even family? This is a question that involves some thought if you have not had thoughts about it before. Boundaries are a strategy to guard your heart and to remain receptive to the voice of God. Boundaries are meant as a source of protection and guide to remain level headed.

There are a host of questions that you will be working through in the practical application section, so we will not address them here, but I would encourage you to begin exploring if you have not already. As we move forward, proceed with an open heart as these practical tips are provided in love and with love with the intent to guide you on your individual journeys at whichever stage you may be in as you read this book. Allow us to begin at the moment of introduction. Are you ready? Let's go!

So you are at...Now, let us backtrack here. I have not always made the best decisions when it came to love, lust, sex, and everything in between. Let us be open in this dialogue. I have placed myself in physically, emotionally, spiritually, and sexually unsafe situations many times, and only by the grace of God that I am here to write before you today. Some I lived out physical consequences that left me with having medical procedures and becoming physically ill. Others left emotional scars and spiritual strongholds that have had to be closed to avoid attachments to generations after me.

At the point of introduction, there are certain boundaries that are most comfortable to you that may not apply to others and their relationships and vice versa. There are various ways of meeting a prospective romantic interest, such as online dating sites, through friends, through church and ministry, work, blind dates, or casual meeting while out. Recommendations are merely suggestions, and I would strongly urge you to pray before making any decisions. Pray for the ability to recognize when God has presented someone of valor and true godly character. I would not recommend meeting or carrying with a relationship with someone you have met at a club or the like as a believing woman. I would suggest getting out and enjoying life. I remember a former male friend told me years ago that I should wait to purchase my home, travel, or essentially live life as a single woman because I should wait to be married before meeting these life markers. After I laughed, rolled my eyes, and laughed again, I replied that I would do no such thing. But the reality is many of us women do just that. The thoughts of, "I will not buy my house until I meet a man." or "I will not travel until I get married because I do not want to go alone." or how about this one, "I will not start my business, go after the job I want, finish my degree, or even have or adopt children until I'm married." This is not to discredit the joys and sanctity of marriage, but we must get out of the mindset that our lives begin or end when we marry. The truth is that our lives begin when we give our lives to Christ, establish our identity in Him, make Him the Lord and Savior of every aspect of our lives. Yes, step out of your comfort zone and live life. Travel with a group of friends or a traveling group for added fun and safety. Buy the house that you wanted to buy. Start your business. Be involved in ministry. How about starting the ministry? Live life abundantly, enjoy this season of singleness as Paul speaks to the people of Corinth, "Now to the unmarried and the widows I say: It is good for them to stay unmarried, as I do" (1 Corinthians 7:8).

Getting back to meeting a potential suitor and the concept of who should approach whom. There is debate on whether it is godly to approach a man of interest first compared to waiting for him to do so. I have my personal views. I would encourage you to pray about whether to approach a man first as I do not agree with a woman doing so. I do believe that it is appropriate to let a man who has expressed interest in you know whether those feelings are reciprocated or if you are not interested beyond friendship. As a modest woman, it is uncouth to lead a man on, to tease or play with his thoughts and emotions under any circumstances, especially when you have no intentions of pursuing a romantic relationship. The next question is whether you should provide your phone number or not and who should ask first. So many rules. The truth is that it depends on you and how the Holy Spirit guides you.

Once the formalities of how you meet potential suitors have been addressed, let us address how one dresses for the date, should he pick you up, how to prepare, and delving into deeper considerations such as when it is best to introduce children and other topics to discuss. When it comes to your attire, it should be according to the location. Again, of modest taste. I am not saying to wear baggy pants or a long dress to your feet and sleeves to your knuckles unless that is your personal style and according to your personal convictions. It is appropriate to dress trendy and attire that you feel attractive and confident in without showing excess. As a voluptuous woman myself, I take extra care in ensuring that I am not showing cleavage, excessive cleavage, that my blouses or dresses are not so low that I cannot bend and that my assets cannot be accessed or seen, whether I am sitting, standing, getting in or out of my car, or modestly bending down if I drop an item.

The next consideration involves whether to allow your gentleman friend to pick you up. Getting to know someone, I am not one to encourage that your suitor picks you up at your home. If you have children, this definitely adds another element into the story. I would strongly urge women to meet their suitor at the location of their date and continue to do so, and especially more so if you do not have history with this individual or if this is first or one of your first times meeting from being an online acquaintance. I recall meeting a man once and although I drove my own car to the location of our date, I made the mistake of agreeing to join him in his car after him continuously saying, "It doesn't make sense that we take two cars to every place." He later drove me to a hotel in another city than where I left my car. Not a good idea, so, sister, I am not sharing suggestions that I have not personally learned from. You may ask at what point is it appropriate for him to meet you at your home or at his home? When you say *I do*, that would be an appropriate time. Okay, this may be somewhat facetious, but making this decision should not be taken lightly. You should know yourself and what your temptations are, and you should be mindful of your suitor's temptations and not placing him in a compromising situation either. This is not to say that he should not be responsible or accountable for his behavior, but you both should be of godly encouragement to each other. If you are praying about doing this God's way, I would encourage you and your prospective courtship partner to pray both individually and as a couple about the timing of relationship markers.

Are there certain topics to steer away from? When is it appropriate to bring up certain subjects? It is always a good thing to let it be known that you have children and your single status from the very beginning. I hear stories when men and women make such comments as, "It just wasn't the right time" or "It wasn't important" or "Let me make sure it's all good before I bring that up" or "It's complicated." I do not agree with this stance. It is never a bad time to share that you have children or your status as a single. If there is more involved, it may not be appropriate to disclose deep-rooted issues, concerns, challenges within the first two minutes of sitting down as for some people, it may have a negative outcome. However, there is a caveat here. There are times when there is a mutual level of unconditional regard and acceptance, there is a godly connection, and you both feel comfortable sharing certain things about yourselves early on. That is wonderful. Remember to guard your heart, spirit, and as a mother, protect your home, your children, and their hearts and spirit.

Speaking of children, when is the right time to introduce your children to your significant other? When is it appropriate for you to meet your significant other's children? When is it appropriate for both your children and his children to meet? Is it ever appropriate to be introduced or have conversations with the mother of your significant other's children or for your significant other to meet the father of your children? Are you squirming in your seat with a hint of anxiety? I sincerely hope not, but these are crucial questions to ask when determining the timing of milestones in your relationship. Again, it is important upon first conversation to disclose that you have children. However, is it wise to introduce your children upon the first date? No. Please be mindful of where your child is developmentally and apply it to the appropriateness and readiness of children.

Let us explore a commonly used theory often applied in the healthcare profession and social sciences: Erikson's Stages of the Life Cycle (1959). Erikson proposed that life occurs in eight stages, capturing the infant years through the older adult years. For purposes of this discussion, we will concentrate on the first six stages: Trust versus Mistrust, Autonomy versus Shame and Doubt, Initiative versus Guilt, Industry versus Inferiority, and Identity versus Role Confusion. The stages discuss what may be typically observed cognitively and emotionally as one transitions through stages and ages.

Beginning in the Trust versus Mistrust stage, the infant begins to establish and maintain trust of others, especially the primary caregivers, to meet their personal needs. When trust of the primary caregivers is developed in a healthy manner, the infant learns to develop trust in others. When mistrust develops, such as in the instance when continuous neglect of feeding the child occurs, lack of healthy emotional attachment, or feeling unsafe with the primary caregiver, the child's trust of others as they develop into adulthood may be negatively impacted. Be mindful of who you choose to have around your children. Although children of this age are very young, negative actions by those who are around them continue to have an impact in their lives. Consistency of trusting, loving, healthy, safe, and secure relationships are invaluable.

The Autonomy versus Shame and Doubt stage involves allowing toddlers to explore their surroundings and develop a sense of independence, understanding that it is healthy for them to want to venture off into their environment with the parents and loved ones there for guidance to prevent injuries. When the primary caregivers do not allow their toddlers the ability to explore their environment or react with discouragement, the toddler may develop feelings of shame and self-doubt, questioning their own abilities and lowering their self-esteem. The third stage, Initiative versus Guilt, occurs in the preschool years when the child learns to and is encouraged to make age-appropriate decisions. The goal is to encourage children to take initiative. However, when children are criticized for taking initiative, being assertive, or when parents exhibit an overbearing approach, guilt may develop in the child.

Stage four occurs in the early school-aged years and is characterized by Industry versus Inferiority. Children are observed and encouraged to grow in their independence. They begin to learn about themselves, and while doing so, begin to compare themselves with their peers. As they do so, they further develop self-confidence. If the child has not achieved certain milestones or abilities as their peers, the child begins to develop feelings of inferiority. Or in the instances that the parent or primary caregiver does not encourage those milestones or the child is ridiculed for not having the same abilities or level of abilities as his or her peers, this may develop into an inferiority complex. How does this relate to your dating or the prospect of being in a romantic relationship? Your child may be vying for your attention, and seeing their mother being entertained by another, especially someone they may not know well, may pose some unique challenges that can be resolved with patience, time, and effort on both you and your significant other. This is a fragile time and may be addressed with tact, respect, and with God's guidance.

Now we move into the stage pertaining to adolescence, Identity versus Role Confusion. The infamous teen years can be an interesting time for anyone, but can present some additional considerations for the dating and courting parent. This is a time when your adolescent is learning about themselves. It is a time of exploration and time to develop their sense of identity through determining the priorities in life. This is a time when they strive to develop their identity while striving to either adhere to the expectations of their parents or break away from the expectations of parents and peers. When this dilemma occurs, an inconsistent identity can result in poor self-concept. How does your child's developmental stage as a teenager impact appropriate boundaries with your significant other? This is a time when it is important to know when and how to introduce this topic to your teen. So often, I have seen single parents pretend for months and longer that they have this "other" life away from their children as a way to "protect" their child, but it appears more of a strategy to protect themselves and avoid any fears that may be inside of them as a parent venturing on this new journey. Our children are intelligent and exhibit a level of emotional intelligence as yourself, with the ability to pick up on cues, observe every behavior, and develop their own thoughts.

It is imperative that all those involved in the child's care are on the same page. This support system includes you as the mother, father if involved, and all others involved in the parenting and guardian responsibilities.

Although children are resilient, let us remember that it is our hope to guard their hearts from forming immature and ungodly attachments in these formative years. It is hoped that the topic of children and the aforementioned questions should be discussed after you and your acquaintance have become more romantically serious. This topic should be one that you and your now significant other should approach with care and in prayer among you, him, and God at the head and center. Engaging in a spiritual fast may be a wonderful way to come together and seek godly wisdom.

Once you and your significant other are on one accord with God in His timing pertaining to the children, you may proceed with how God leads. Over the years, it has hurt my heart when I see children prematurely introduced to a woman's significant other, especially when the gentleman is not a significant other, but merely an acquaintance. She would soon discover his intentions and abruptly end the communication. Yes, the woman may be well and hopefully had developed a healthy way of coping with and moving forward from the situation. But have we thought about the children and the emotional attachment that they have developed? Although, it may be a shallow and short-lived attachment, nonetheless, an emotional attachment to the gentleman has occurred. And while the mother has moved on within days or weeks, depending on the age and developmental stage of the child, the child may struggle with no longer seeing this person, and more than likely does not understand the reason. Do not use this as an opportunity to insult, demean, or belittle the gentleman, especially to or in front of your child. This is an unhealthy way of coping from a break up. There is a term used in social sciences referred to as operant conditioning or may commonly be described as observational learning. What does this term mean? Essentially, it is the principle that people, especially children, learn from *observing* or watching others. Children observe, even subconsciously, our mannerisms, the dynamics between and among people, how we interact with those around us, differences in how we present in the world compared to how we are at home, inconsistencies, how we cope with challenging situations, and our overall behaviors. Those who know me know that I often make the following statement, "How my son treats his wife in the future will be predicated upon how I allow a man to treat me today." Remember, my beloved sister, our children watch us more than you realize.

This also refers to the type of emotional attachment that our children engage in, such as how we allow our children to speak to or refer to the man we are becoming better acquainted.

Celibacy: Conveniently Celibate and True Celibacy

A natural segue from boundaries is to discuss the lifestyle of celibacy and abstinence. What is the difference between the two? Celibacy is generally a choice that one engages in to refrain from any form of sexual activity, often associated with fulfilling faith-based vows as a single person. And it is fulfilled upon marriage. Abstinence is used within two contexts. In the sex education world, schools, and within social sciences, the term is used as a form of sexual contraception for adolescents to refrain from engaging in sexual acts until they are ready or are properly informed. This form of abstinence may or may not be related to religious views. Abstinence, within a second context, is often used to refrain from an enjoyable activity for a certain amount of time. We often see abstinence applied within the realm of spiritual fasting. A married couple may abstain from sexual activity for a short amount of time as a form of spiritual fasting together. One may abstain from food or social media in today's era, or any activity that the individual feels distracts them from focusing on God.

Loneliness versus Being Alone

What is your motive behind desiring a relationship? Is it with the desire for marriage? Is it for the desire for companionship or partnership? Is it to fulfill fleshly desires, such as sex, filling a void, or loneliness? Let us speak to loneliness for a moment. Loneliness is a true experience, one that is experienced by each of us at one time or another, in different seasons. God has created us as people to be in connection with one another. We are not meant to do life alone, but in collaboration, partnership, and in community. This is the difference between being alone and loneliness. Do you believe that there is a difference between the two? What characterizes each? Both are an experience in and of itself. Being alone is being by yourself and having the ability to function in a healthy manner. It is understanding that you are able to move about your space and move about your life without reservations or qualms. And in some cases, even moving about in fear, yet having enough faith of a mustard seed to walk alone. The focus is in moving confidently and victoriously in God. Experiencing moments of loneliness may be a normal part of life, but be mindful of the length of time and negative thoughts and behaviors that accompany it. It is experienced, whereas when experiencing a state of loneliness, it can be debilitating. Has a sense of fear or discomfort been allowed to take root in your life, hindering you from living and experiencing life? Has a sense of jealousy or even envy set in as you look into and observe the lives of your friends and your loved ones? Loneliness is when you believe and live your life less than full capacity because of being alone It may involve low self-esteem, poor self-image, or may involve feelings of depressed mood, major depressive disorder, or a form of anxiety, or that sense of isolation may lead to thoughts of suicide or wanting to self-harm.

Influence of Others: Societal, Family, and Cultural Pressures

Perhaps your motive behind desiring a relationship is not loneliness, but at the influence of others. I recall some years ago, I was mentoring a young mother. She was in her early twenties at the time. She had recently given birth to her second child. The father of the children was described as being intermittently involved in both her life and the lives of their children. Both parties were very young. This is not to discount the role of accountability and responsibility, however; hopefully, a sense of maturity and wisdom comes as we get older. And the lack of inner maturity appeared to play a role with this couple. The couple had dissolved their relationship on several occasions with the most recent being at her choice. We were speaking on the phone when she shared a recent conversation between her and her mother. She resided with her parents, her two children, and her younger siblings. This young lady mentioned that she had started chatting with an old boyfriend who resided in another state who made his intentions known of wanting to rekindle what they once had. She found herself in a unique dilemma. Should she pursue this old flame proclaiming to give her the world in another state or should she return to a relationship with the father of her children, one in which she believed was rooted from a domineering nature? The young woman shared that her mother encouraged her to move out-of-state with the young children and pursue a relationship with her former boyfriend. I could hear the anxiety and uncertainty in her young voice. I dared her to explore one option she did not know was an alternative: to not become romantically involved with anyone and work on her and the life she wished to create for her children with God front and center. I shared with her what we must proclaim to our younger sisters and daughters. Her mother as with many others, perhaps in your life as well, have pure and genuine intentions when they encourage a young woman to date or not to date. I asked her to take out a piece of paper as we spoke into the night, and asked her what did she want out of life for herself and her children? What were her goals, both long-term and short-term goals? Where did she see herself in one year, five years, or ten years? And if getting married was a part of that plan, would any part of her goals be different if she were not married within the time frame that she set for herself? Her response was, "I never thought of that." I said, "Well, tonight at 11:35, is just as good as any other moment to start thinking about it." As she shared her goals, the intonation changed, and she sounded more sure of what she desired. She was not working at the time and did not have a car, these were the basics of everyone's need. She began to share that she wanted to work. So I asked, "Okay, what kind of work?" She replied, then followed with a list of "I want...I want..." I would not let it go. I questioned every statement. I challenged every idea with question terms, such as how? What for? How long would that take? Have you researched what that program may entail? What about childcare? Have you discussed these ideas with you parents before or with the father of your children to develop a schedule? Have you researched economical cars, the amount you need to put down, what is your credit score, and if you had to have a cosigner, do you have someone willing to do so? We discussed how to categorize each long-term goal into manageable and attainable short-term goals, and divided the short-term goals into weekly, and in some cases, daily goals to be successful. By the time the conversation came to a close, she had developed a God-confident approach, a strategy, and accountability in achieving those goals. But primarily, she developed a plan where she was no longer feeling as though she had to be dependent on the father of her children or a relationship with a man to succeed and knew that she could provide a godly future for herself and her children. We concluded with prayer, and one year after that conversation, she was working on strengthening her relationship with God, working on a positive co-parenting relationship with the father, developing her parenting skills, working two jobs, transitioning into one job, had purchased a vehicle, and was contributing to her parents' household financially, and providing childcare for her siblings along with her own children.

Why did I share this story about the influence of others? Sometimes, the influence of others may encourage us to place ourselves in situations that God would not otherwise have for us. I believe as parents, as friends, as family, we want the absolute best for our children and loved ones. But we must be careful how we speak into their lives, what and how we encourage them. Sometimes it may be our desire and not God's desire for that individual's life. When it comes to single men and women and the topic of marriage, there appears to be a double standard as women are oftentimes portrayed as "something" is wrong or somehow denoting that it is her fault for her singleness. Perhaps she is too aggressive and masculine. Perhaps she needs to be a little more like "this" or a little more like "that." As a society, as a culture, and sometimes within families, we teach our daughters that they must change to be considered desirable. Truly speaking, there are things that God will call us to do in preparation, and we will discuss that in this chapter, but generally speaking, to suggest that the woman is at 100% to blame for singleness is a far stretch.

The reality for many of us is that getting married is not the problem; it is marrying the one whom God has called us to marry. Can we be real ladies? Now, what about for us older women who are in our mid-thirties and older? My goodness, the lovely statements that have been made by loved ones, acquaintances, and people who I do not know who have shared insight on my life of singleness. I have had someone attempt to introduce me to a man who was in a coma (and she disclosed this very important fact during prayer). I have had someone introduce me to someone who was 32 years my senior. If this is appropriate in your life, I shed no judgment. This is, however, not what God has called in my life. I have had a man who was having auditory hallucinations related to a mental health disorder track me down while jogging at the park. I have had someone tell me that once I graduated with my doctorate, it was time to meet someone because I did not want to spend my older years alone. And I have people imply that my standards were too high, not high enough, or non-existent.

I share these stories lightheartedly. But I share, nonetheless, to let you know that our loved ones, hopefully, and most cases sincerely, mean well as they desire to see us happy, but we must remember being with someone should not make one feel complete or feel whole as though those of us single ones have been walking on earth as incomplete beings. God is more than an enhancement or supplement to us. He is our portion. He completes us. No longer walk from a place of feeling as though that void or empty space in your spirit needs to be filled with sex, food, friendship, relationship, addictions, or with the need of approval. That empty space where you feel as though you are missing something or something is just not right; beloved, know that is Jesus knocking on the door of your heart, saying, "Daughter, that piece that is still untouched, that door that remains closed to Me, yes, that area in your life. Daughter, bring it to Me. You have carried it long enough. You are enough, with your flaws and all, you are beautiful and I love you. It's time to let Me love you, heal you, restore, and give life more abundantly if you would let down your guard with Me, surrender it all to Me, be vulnerable with Me. You're not mess. You are a vessel that I will work through if you allow Me to."

It is time, sister. What is the desire of your heart? Remember to *delight yourself in the Lord and He will grant you the desires of your heart* (Psalm 37:4). With this said, it is okay to say that you desire marriage, a God-filled and God-designed marriage. Marriage is ministry, so when desiring a mate, ask yourself if this is the person you see yourself doing, walking out, and living ministry with. Do not feel ashamed to share your heart truth. But in this heart truth, remember to be prayerful, humble, and obedient to God's instructions. Do not allow this desire to be bred from a place of desperation, as that opens the door for plans that God may not have intended for you. Is it hard to lead this life of celibacy and godly obedience? Yes, it is hard, and there are times when I ask why am I in this position. Then God places His hand on my heart, and I bring my brokenness to Him, my pieces, my tears, my flaws, my desires and He makes a beautiful masterpiece, message, and testimony. He reminds me that not only how my son treats his wife is predicated upon how I allow a man to treat me today, but just as importantly, How God's daughters live their lives may be influenced by how I choose to let God's light shine on mine. That is a deep revelation and a profound responsibility. Stay true ,my sister, and in God's timing, your husband will be presented and revealed. Allow God to prepare you as He deems necessary.

Practical Application

Several concepts were discussed in this chapter. I suppose the most important place to begin this application journey is to discuss your personal boundaries and standards that you have set into place as a way to guard your heart and to remain receptive to the voice of God. As it pertains to courting, this may require a paradigm shift from what you may have done in the past and the conscious decision on how you are going to proceed from this point forward. What are your thoughts about introducing your children to your significant other? What are your thoughts about when the right time is to tell your new acquaintance that you have children? Should they be allowed to your home? When your kids are present, when should your significant other be allowed to your home? When are they not? How long has it been since you were in a relationship? Was it a relationship or a situationship? Was your last relationship your marriage or perhaps a long-term relationship where your children were actively involved and knew of your significant other well? Explore your past relationships, your feelings, current emotions, thoughts, behaviors that evolved from those past relationships. If you are in a relationship, how did you address these questions or are you addressing them at all? When is the best time to meet your significant other's children? At what point is it appropriate for your children to join you on family outings and dates? At what point is it appropriate for your children to call your significant other more than their name and establish names that have more of an emotional attachment such as "Dad?" Or is it ever? Does the age of your children and if he has children, matter on when and how you move forward? There are a barrage of questions to explore, more than what you are reading here. My intent is not to confuse you or cause anxiety or overwhelm you, but to open that door of communication between you and God, between you and your current or future significant other, and how you would begin to approach this topic.

In the next section, I provide Scriptures that have and continue to speak to me in the preparation stage. Meditate on them, share with other single women, and know that God has your back and your heart. After spending time journaling on how these verses come to life for you, let us end in prayer.

Applicable Scriptures

"But perfect love drives out fear, because fear has to do with punishment. The one who fears is not made perfect in love. We love because He first loved us" (1 John 4:18-19).

"Don't just pretend to love others. Really love them. Hate what is wrong. Hold tightly to what is good. Love each other with genuine affection, and take delight in honoring each other" (Romans 12:9-10).

"Love is patient, love is kind. It does not envy, it does not boast, it is not proud. It does not dishonor others, it is not self-seeking, it is not easily angered, it keeps no record of wrongs" (1 Corinthians 13:4-5).

"I pray that your love will overflow more and more, and that you will keep on growing in knowledge and understanding" (Philippians 1:9).

"Let us not love with words or speech but with actions and in truth" (1 John 3:18).

"The Lord is my Portion, says my soul. Therefore, I hope in Him" (Lamentations 3:24).

"She confidently trusts the Lord to take care of her" (Psalm 112:7).

"There will be people in your life who will claim to love you, but will turn their back on you when it is no longer convenient for them. Thankfully, there is one who promises I will never leave you nor forsake you" (Hebrews 13:5).

"He cares for those who trust Him" (Nahum 1:7)

"The one who trusts in the Lord is protected" (Proverbs 29:25).

"No temptation has overtaken you that is not common to man. God is faithful, and He will not let you be tempted beyond your ability, but with the temptations He will also provide the way of escape, that you may be able to endure it" (Corinthians 10:13).

Prayer

Father, I bring my beautiful sister, God's masterpiece made to perfection to You, God. We have entered this journey of self-discovery, and most importantly, God-discovery. God, we boldly bow down at Your feet and although hard at times, we put aside our plans and submit to Your plan for us and our family. We humbly ask that You purge old patterns, thoughts, and associated emotions, feelings of rejection, the need to please and seek approval, past hurts of sexual abuse, psychological abuse, and physical abuse that has left a scar in the core of our hearts. Every time my sister enters a new relationship or friendship, becoming either too guarded and cold, or easily attached and codependent, it pulls the scab of a never-healed wound, causing re-traumatization. We ask You to pull back the layers and heal Your daughter's heart, from the core to the surface. May my sister move past the fear and choose vulnerability. May she choose to be vulnerable to You and surrender *every* realm of her life to You, including her love life. May she enter this love journey with You leading it, showing her what You desire for her to know and grow in. From this moment forward, we humbly surrender to You, Heavenly Father. Have Your way in our lives, Lord. May we be vessels of Your light, love, strength and wisdom. Amen.

Part Three

When Clarity Comes

By now, we have discussed many areas of your life as you venture through your co-parenting with Christ journey. Congratulations for allowing yourself to explore, to reflect, to dig deep, to war to get to this place of moving towards harmony in your life and ultimately within your family and home. We have discussed your identity in Christ, what you have been called to do in life, how to triumphantly persevere, your home and parenting, healing parent wounds, the mindset, and dating and courtship. You have put in the work through reading, journaling, fasting, discussion, studying your sword of God, and allowing yourself to sit in a place of surrender and vulnerability. This, sister, is the journey of healing and peace so that in the future when situations arise that feel more like chaos, you can stand in the midst of the storm and still feel God's presence and peace evermore clearly. But before going any further, now it is time for the next part of this journey: how to recognize the voice of God, what to do, and how all of these pieces come together to bring you positive emotional well-being.

Chapter 8

Hearing the Voice of God and Being Obedient

"My sheep hear My voice, and I know them, and they follow Me"
(John 10:27).

CO-PARENTING WITH CHRIST AS A SINGLE
parent can be challenging at times, but it is not impossible. With
the concepts discussed thus far, you may not experience the true
impact of healing, restoration, harmony, and peace if you are
unable to recognize the voice of God and how to respond when
you are called upon to move. This next chapter speaks to just
that. We live in a world that says when you speak to God or
feel His presence or hear a gentle whisper in your spirit, that
it is unhealthy and peculiar. Do not be dismayed. Do not allow
anyone to deter you from having a relationship with God. Do
not allow others to make you feel ashamed, guilty, or confused.
Hearing the voice of God is similar to a muscle. It may feel unique
and different initially because it is unfamiliar. As time continues,
you begin to strengthen this muscle, which is the ability to hear.
This muscle is strengthened through Bible reading and studying,
through being spiritually in-tune with God, through prayer,
through fasting, journaling, and introspection because you are
developing a pure intimacy with the One who created you.

Obedience Is Better than Sacrifice

One morning, several years ago, as a recent born-again believer, my son and I had just arrived late to the second church service. Hurriedly, I dropped my son in children's ministry and I quickly walked towards the main sanctuary as the teaching portion of service had begun minutes before. I remember it being an absolutely gorgeous day with a touch of warmth, flowers were blooming, and there was a casual silence on the church grounds. I decided to sit on a bench located in one of the outdoor corridors so I may take in the beauty of the day while allowing the Word to minister to my spirit. As I pulled my Bible, pen, and notebook out, I remember thanking God for such a beautiful moment.

Suddenly, I saw a woman, man, and two children in the corridor. The woman was frantically following behind the man who had two children. He quickly walked past me, up the corridor, telling the children to walk directly next to him, while the woman was trying to get his attention. The man sternly spoke to the woman to leave him and the kids alone. He told her to leave them at the church, and as soon as she would leave church, he may begin spending quality time with the children on church grounds. It was apparent that the two were once a couple who gave birth to two beautiful children. It appeared that they were attempting to co-parent and find a feasible way of doing this that was convenient and had minimal disruption in their children's lives. I instantly came out of my Sunday glow and realized what was occurring. I did not want to appear as though I noticed, so I began looking into my Bible, pretending to read it. It was an awkward moment that I thought would pass so I may return to listening to the sermon through the intercom. The couple continued to hash out their dispute through the outdoor patio. I had assumed that it was resolved. Shortly thereafter, the two reappeared. The woman appeared embarrassed, so I graciously smiled at her before looking down at my Bible. Then suddenly a voice from nowhere said, "Go pray with her." I did not know who spoke suddenly and quietly to me. I began to assume that perhaps I was not getting as much rest as I thought I was. So I dismissed this *thought*.

The man continued to tell the mother of their children to leave them, go to work, and return to the church later that evening to pick the children up. She replied with a gentle, "Please, I will take you and the girls wherever you want to go. But please, I cannot leave you and the girls here. What if they are hungry? If they have to use the restroom? Please, I will not leave them here all day. Please allow me to take you guys wherever you would like to go. To your home? To your family, and I'll come pick them up after. I can't go to work knowing that they're going to be here for the rest of the afternoon and no one else is here." The frustration and the worry of a mother's heart could be heard in her voice, seen in her disposition, and in her pace, as she tirelessly followed her two daughters and their father. The two verbally danced for the duration of the hour. And again, I heard it, "Go pray with her." I suddenly realized that it was God speaking to me, commanding that I pull the young mother aside and pray with her. I felt incompetent. I felt insecure. Yet, God called me to complete a task. He chose to use me as a vessel for His assignment to be carried through. I remember *telling* God, "I'm not ready. What do I say?" And God replied, "I will give you the words. Go pray with her." I dragged along. I sat there on the same bench and looked for her and the children. They were nowhere to be found. I said, "Lord, I am scared, but the next time I see her, I will walk up to her and pray for her." I was content in my mediocre plan and rehearsed continuously in my mind of how I may approach her. I sat on that bench for the remaining time of service, waiting for the family to cross my path again. Church service ended, and

I walked to my son's classroom to pick him up. I had rationalized, "Okay, Lord, I guess the problem was resolved and I did not need to pray with her after all." As my son and I walked down the corridor towards the parking lot, I looked up and saw the young mother sitting on a bench hunched over comfortably in the arms of another woman who had her hands on the mother's back, praying with her.

At that very moment, a sense of guilt and shame came over me. A moment of fear, of shallowness, and of selfishness on my part could have ruined a moment to witness to someone and to intercede on behalf of someone. I sat in my car and experienced a rush of emotions fill my heart, with tears welling in my eyes and a resounding "I'm sorry, God" flowing from my mouth. "I'm sorry" for not trusting God in the moment, for not being okay with not knowing the plan, for not moving when He said to move, and for putting my needs over His children. God softly corrected His daughter by saying, "It's not for you, it is for others that when I call you, when I command you to move, you must trust that I have a plan." I realized that when it comes to His children, God's will will always be done, whether I feel ready or not. His plan will not stop because I choose not to fulfill it. He will search until He finds the one who is willing to fulfill His purpose. The one who is vulnerable. The one who surrenders their plan for His.

When God Speaks, You Listen

What situations in your life has God spoken to you and you chose not to listen? Or perhaps you doubted that was the voice of God? You questioned whether it was God's voice, your own, people, or another source. As mentioned earlier in the book, God's Word and instruction are pure. It may not feel like the easiest, most comfortable, or even the most convenient route, but it is the most righteous and just path. God will never speak against His Word, for the Word is God. His Word empowers, heals, uplifts, restores, redeems, encourages, comforts, and brings peace and joy, among others. His Word does not bring harm upon people

It can be intimidating at times, but know that when God calls you forth, God knows what He is doing, why He is doing, and the time in which He has called you. When in God, you must keep yourself in a place to understand and recognize the many ways that God speaks to you. It may be through dreams in the middle of the night, through visions consisting of words or images that suddenly appear visually, through the words spoken by those in your circle of influence, through the Scripture, that subtle voice in your spirit, or that gut feeling or instinct that we know as the Holy Spirit guiding us. It is important to recognize His voice, but even more critical to be obedient to what He has called you to and when He said to. So your question may be, how do you listen to His voice? Perhaps the even bigger question should be how do you act or move after hearing His voice? Let us refer to His Word, *For God has not instilled a spirit of fear, but of love, power, and of sound mind"* (2 Timothy 1:7). Move, move, move. Never second-guess the power of God. Never second-guess the power of moving forward. Use what you already have at your disposal. When God asked you to move, He has already provided what you need to move forward as He has called you.

Practical Application

I would like for you to take a moment with your journal nearby and ask God to show you times, situations, and experiences when He spoke to you and either you were unsure if it was Him speaking to you or if you were able to recognize His voice, you chose to follow a different. Why so harsh, you might say? Or, Chanel, why do you insist that it was by choice? Because to grow in our relationship with anyone especially with God, it is imperative to hold ourselves accountable when we are wrong. It is important to understand when we made a decision against God's instruction. It is in this act of acknowledgment that we may ask for forgiveness, repent, or in other words, turn away from the wrongful act, and allow God to reveal to us the steps and patterns that led to that choice. When you are in a place of vulnerability and surrender, and God reveals these steps to you, you may learn how to open your heart to the voice of God. Think about how God has spoken to you over the years. His voice never changes as He is the same yesterday, today, and forevermore, but how you recognize His voice may only strengthen as you draw nearer to Him.

Countless Scriptures are referred to when conducting a thorough study on hearing the voice of God. I selected a few verses that I have especially embraced over the years. Read each Scripture and remember to open your Bible and read the entire section or chapter to grasp the full context. After you have completed this task and journaled on how to apply these Scriptures in your life, end this chapter in prayer as God prepares you for our next chapter together.

Applicable Scriptures

"Call to Me and I will answer you, and will tell you great and hidden things that you have not known" (Jeremiah 33:3).

"Your own ears will hear Him. Right behind you a voice will say, 'This is the way you should go,'" whether to the right or to the left" (Isaiah 30:21).

"When the Spirit of truth comes, He will guide you into all truth. He will not speak on His own but will tell you what He has heard. He will tell you about the future" (John 16:13).

"The Spirit alone gives eternal life. Human effort accomplishes nothing. And the very words I have spoken to you are spirit and life" (John 6:63).

"Anyone who belongs to God listens gladly to the words of God" (John 8:47).

"Blessed rather are those who hear the word of God and keep it" (Luke 11:28).

"I will instruct you and teach you in the way you should go; I will counsel you with My loving eye on you" (Psalm 32:8).

Prayer

Father, as we come humbly to the Throne of Grace, we ask for discernment to recognize Your voice, wisdom to know when to move, and strength to move even if in the midst of fear. May we hear Your voice and remember that You have not instilled a spirit of fear, but of love, power, and of sound mind. We thank you for preparing us, guiding us, and entrusting us as Your vessels for Your light to shine through, Your love to resonate through, and Your assignment to flow through. In Jesus' name, we pray this, amen.

Chapter 9

Finding Harmony
in the Midst of the Chaos

"Whoever is of God listens to God. Those who belong to God hear the words of God. This is the reason that you do not listen to those words, to Me because you do not belong to God and are not of God or in harmony with Him" (John 8:47).

EMOTIONAL WELL-BEING IS THE LAST PIECE of the puzzle that brings harmony into our lives as women and single mothers of faith. Allow us to first define the terms *well-being* and *emotional well-being* before we delve into a discussion of balance, harmony, and recognizing when an imbalance occurs. The term *well-being*, as defined by Black and Hecklinger (2006), refers to one having a balanced lifestyle and quality of life. It focuses specifically on one's ability to healthfully balance the various roles one plays and the multiple responsibilities or tasks one has, such as religion and spiritual journey, attitude towards life, career, family, and opportunities to learn, and friendships and family. When an imbalance occurs, stress is the result. Emotional well-being is generally defined as an individual's level of quality of life (Black and Hecklinger 2006). According to Deaton and Kahneman (2010), emotional well-being refers to the "emotional quality of an individual's everyday experience." It involves the frequency and intensity of experiences that result in an individual's life being self-reported as pleasant or unpleasant. For purposes of this text, emotional well-being is more specifically defined in the context of psychological well-being.

Some time ago, I recall driving home after a long day of work. I met with several clients earlier in the day and feverishly completed assessments within the required time frame. It was about fifteen minutes before sundown. Tears suddenly began to well up in my eyes and started strolling down my face. It was uncontrollable, to the point where I could no longer see the road before me. I began dabbing my cheeks and wiping the tears from my eyes, hoping that other drivers would not notice. I started to take deep breaths with thoughts roaming through my mind, "Am I freaking out? Is something wrong? Why am I crying? This is so not like me." Earlier in the week, I had received notice that my school of several years was closing, and I had six months to complete my dissertation process, including recruiting for and conducting my doctoral study. My bills were one month behind. As I calmed down and raced to arrive home, I knew that I needed to have time with God. After checking with my son and conversing on how his day went, I went into my bedroom, closed the door, and took a long candlelit bath. Afterward, I laid in my bed with Bible in hand and ready for a long intimate talk with God. This was the third uncontrollable sporadic crying spell that I had within a two-week period. In my time of reflection, I realized that the crying moments were only one symptom. Over the months leading to that time, I had moments of sadness and despair, panic attacks associated with anxiety, digestion issues at an all-time high, bouts of forgetfulness, and difficulty sleeping. I felt overwhelmed and was experiencing burnout. I was frustrated with my current state in life. Although the schooling was an additional stressor, it was no comparison to what I felt within that stage pertaining to my career and where I felt I should have been in life. You see, I was always trying to decide what bill to pay on time, what amount to add to bring certain bills current, and what amount to add onto the bills' checklist for the following month. Life was always on the go with family, work, and ministry. This life had become the new norm for me. I learned how to function. I learned how to function with a mask, portraying that life was good all the time, and I could handle anything that came my way. To the outside world, people would tell me how courageous I was or how I was a great example to women. To me, I was not an anomaly, as I was taking advantage of the open doors, and believed that when driven and willing to do the work, anyone could achieve the same goals. The truth was, I was falling apart at a rate that I could not keep up, explain, or rationalize. I was broken internally, and it was beginning to manifest physically. The level of stress that I was able to cope with in my twenties, and even early thirties, was no longer possible in my mid to late thirties. I knew that I could not continue to navigate life in such an unhealthy way.

"So how do I fix this, Lord?" became the question that I asked God. And with a resounding stance, He responded, "Daughter, be vulnerable, surrender to Me. I've been waiting for you to step aside and allow Me to fix it for you." Do you notice a pattern in this book? If you have not noticed, well, here it is: it involves surrendering to God and allowing Him to fix the broken pieces of my life and make it into a masterpiece

I sat on my bed, closed my eyes, and connected my heart to God's, and said, "God, I get it. Please bring balance to my life." It was at that moment God reminded me of a video I had watched a couple of years before that featured a grad student. Her life philosophy resonated with my spirit. This vibrant woman said there was no such thing as balance, but in harmony, every realm in life falls into place. As I listened to her further, she justified that balance implies a sense of perfection and insinuates that we can devote the same amount of effort, time, and energy into every area, task, situation, and person in our lives. This is impossible. Whereas, the social media influencer went on to say that in harmony, we are able to freely navigate through the various realms in our lives without the pressure of perfection. In harmony, we can give health thirty percent of our time as we create ways to alleviate stress, while removing some time and energy from another area. In harmony, it is a dance of knowing when certain realms, tasks, situations, and people deserve more time, energy, and attention than others, and understanding that this is fluid. This life philosophy changed my perspective, but I never took it a step further to implement in my own life until God brought this concept back to memory.

At that stage in my life, I felt discontent. Grateful, but discontent with where I was in life with the poverty mindset and a job that I believed no longer had the same meaning as it once had years before. A paradigm shift began to take place. God began to peel back layers and took me on a journey where prioritization, listening to God's voice was vital, and making time to be still was a part of my daily routine. I entered a journey that began with a God vision. God whispered the words *present, impactful, intentional* over the next few months, which led to a series that He guided me to introduce to the ladies of the single mothers' ministry.

Present

Have you ever had a moment when you were trying to have a meaningful conversation with your teenager, and the entire time, their face was glued to their cell phone with the occasional "mmm hmmm," "Okay, Mom," or "Yes, Mom, I'm listening" responses? Or your little one is attempting to ask you a question on why butterflies are created with such beautiful colors while you are typing away, answering work-related emails? I am sure you can relate. What are these scenarios missing? Being present. What does *being present* refer to? It means embracing the here and now. It means taking advantage of this very moment and embracing the situation, the person, the feeling, and taking it all in. It means that when your child wants to have a conversation with you, you place the laptop to the side or place your cell phone on silent, sit with him or her, and stare into their eyes as they share what is on their hearts. Perhaps it is setting time aside everyday specifically to respond to emails, answer phone calls, write, and tend to other business-related tasks. When you are in work mode, focus on work. But once that time frame has ceased, it is now time to tend to other realms in your life, including motherhood, your health, your time with God, and your social life. Some may read the last few sentences and say, "How can I just shut down one area of my life and move into the next?" Have you heard the saying that women think like spaghetti and men think like waffles? Men are wired to compartmentalize and women are designed to have every thought, every conversation touch, and are somehow connected. Women have developed the art of starting a conversation with one topic, be on the third topic within twenty minutes, and ending the phone call two hours later, returning to the initial topic without skipping a beat or dropping a sweat. Although simplistic, there appears to be some relevance. You may not shut down one area at a time, but you can *choose* to see what is important at that time, what needs your attention at that moment, and refocus or shift so that those most important to you get to see and spend time with the most precious and conscientious you. This intentional stance allows you to improve your emotional well-being by keeping the most important at focus, guiding you on how and whom you should prioritize in your life. This leads us to intentionality.

Intentional

When you hear the term *intentionality*, what comes to mind? It is the conscious decision to engage with others on purpose, in purpose, and with purpose. What does this look like in your life? It is navigating through life with effort, intention, and making the decision to make the most of every moment. When I examined my life, I began to recognize what I call time-wasters, such as the individuals who want to take from you, harm you, and who generally do not mean you well. I began to notice additional time-wasters, such as distractions with social media scrolling, being on the phone at various times of the evening, and ways to either procrastinate and not address the issue at hand or to emotionally tap out of life for a while. So when harmony was manifested in my life, it resembled not talking on the phone in the evenings when I arrived home from work because that interrupted quality time with my son. Harmony and intentionality meant that on the days that my father picked my son up from school, placing quality time aside of my work day to call my son and inquire about the details of his day. On the days that I was able to pick him up from school or after arriving late from work, having a quality conversation with my son, asking thorough questions of each class period, of assignments due, class assignments and concepts worked on in each of the seven periods, homework, approaching tests, what concepts he had a difficult time grasping and needing additional support and assistance in, and interpersonal conflicts that may have arisen between himself and another peer or disputes among other students, how the situation was addressed, and what may have improved the situation further developing critical thinking skills. Our intentional conversations included questions about concepts that pertain to him as a young man, society, and current events going on in the world. It included humor, profound thought-provoking conversations, questions, and sometimes may have ended in tears or in complete silence. And that was okay because a child, especially a teen who is willing and able to have an open dialogue with their parent, is critical to their development and a healthy part of the growing process.

What am I saying? Strive to be intentional in every relationship. Be conscientious of the words that flow from your mouth for *a good man brings good things out of the good stored up in his heart, and an evil man brings evil things out of the evil stored up in his heart. For the mouth speaks what the heart is full of* (Luke 6:45). How about being aware of the thoughts that not only sporadically enter your mind, but those unhealthy thoughts that you allow to dwell as *we demolish arguments and every pretension that sets itself up against the knowledge of God, and we take captive every thought to make it obedient to Christ* (2 Corinthians 10:5). Be intentional of behaviors we choose to engage in as *no temptation has overtaken you except such as is common to man; but God is faithful, who will not allow you to be tempted beyond what you are able, but with the temptation will also make the way of escape, that you may be able to bear it* (1 Corinthians 10:13).

Explore what intentionality looks like in your life and in your relationships, it is truly a life-changing and life-saving experience.

Impactful

Impact. That word should hopefully evoke powerful emotions in you and in your spirit. At the end of the day, at the end of our lives, at the end of every season and every relationship, understand that it not about you, but about the legacy you leave behind. Yes, we spoke of intentionality, we spoke of being present, yes for us, but to help us in how we engage in the lives of those God has entrusted us to speak into. Influence, contribution, mentorship, leadership, legacy: what thoughts, emotions, and memories come to mind when your eyes glance over these words? Are they taking root yet? Let us try this one on for size. What comes to mind when you think of the Titus two woman? Let us pause for a moment for you to open your Bible and read the Book of Titus, especially as it pertains to both older women and younger women.

"Likewise, teach the older women to be reverent in the way they live, not to be slanderers or addicted to much wine, but to teach what is good. Then they can urge the younger women to love their husbands and children, to be self-controlled and pure, to be busy at home, to be kind, and to be subject to their husbands, so that no one will malign the word of God" (Titus 23-5).

As a woman in her late thirties, I do not take this role and responsibility of a mentor lightly. You may feel that you are not old enough to be a mentor or that you are an older woman who no longer has the right to speak into the lives of others. Nothing could be further from the truth. Perhaps you believe that your past disqualifies you from speaking wisdom into the lives of those who come after you. God has placed you in a position of influence wherever you are in your life. Use what you have in your hands. Use what you have at your disposal. Use what God has placed in your heart. Use the resources and tools that God has equipped you with, dear woman of God. Speak it. Live it. Be it. People are waiting on you. People are waiting on you in your community, in your school, at your job, in your family. How about this? People are waiting for you within your own household. Ensure that when you have answered to the call of duty and responded to the task at hand, that you are not spewing hatred, that you are not spewing negative energy, that you are not releasing toxins into your sister's heart, so pray if there are areas in your life that require healing; please address that or begin to address before venturing into the space of mentorship and leadership.

What are you doing to impact, influence, and contribute to a dying world? What has God placed in you specifically to reach, connect, and bring together His children? Remember, all of us have been created with a God gift meant to be used to add to the body of Christ. My beloved sister, do not sit on the gift that has been bestowed upon you. Use it for His glory. And in the midst, you will begin to notice, as research indicates, that a heart of giving and generous spirit has beneficial implications. According to Bea (2016), the act of giving not only helps others, but is proven to boost physical and mental health, such as lowering blood pressure, increasing self-esteem, lowering the risk of depression or depressed moods (increasing serotonin), lowering stress hormones, such as cortisol, and overall life longevity. Be a woman of generous intentions as it not only benefits your emotional well-being, but creates an environment of love, and a legacy of positivity and giving.

Support

To move in a place of intentionality, impact, and presence, on this quest to emotional well-being, one must develop a support system. As we discussed in previous chapters, support is vital in this journey of motherhood. During my doctoral study, I found that the presence of support was a crucial piece to not only how we parent our children, but beneficial to our emotional well-being as mothers. An association exists between the presence of support and type of support with positive emotional well-being. My study on the emotional well-being of single mothers who identified as Christian found that positive emotional well-being was observed within three types of support: physical, emotional, and social.

Physical

Physical support entails the tangible types of assistance the single mother requires to function well within her role as a mother while improving her sense of emotional well-being. By tangible, I am referring to types of assistance that may require paid or non-paid supports, such as financial assistance, transportation, childcare, or perhaps assistance with contributing towards or paying a bill, rent, or mortgage payment. When receiving physical support, it alleviates a considerable amount of stress that is felt both financially and emotionally. Or knowing that a friend or family member is willing to provide childcare for low to no cost alleviates the stress of needing to work while knowing that your children are cared for.

Physical Signs of Disharmony

My goal with this section is to assist in promoting positive physical well-being by equipping you with the tools to recognize when your body is responding poorly to disharmony and imbalance in your life. What are the physical symptoms that you have experienced during a challenging season in your life? Shortness of breath, anxiety, panic attacks, depressed mood, difficulty falling or staying asleep, memory concerns or difficulty concentrating, weight gain or weight loss to name a few. Sound familiar? You may feel as though you are running or functioning on mere fumes. As you are moving through challenging times in your life, it is important to monitor these physical symptoms by maintaining a log or keeping a record to document the type of physical symptoms, the intensity and severity of the symptoms, such as, do you feel it is life threatening, how often you experience them, and triggers, such as noting under which circumstances or situations do you experience these physical symptoms.

As you will find with both physical and emotional symptoms, when you document the details of these occurrences, you will be able to develop healthy coping mechanisms for when you encounter future trials.

As your mindset begins to shift gears and you develop the ability to recognize disharmony, you must train your mind in recognizing when the physical symptoms have developed. What are steps that you may take to recognize and ultimately address the physical aspect of the journey? I would recommend seeking medical advice and attention from a creditable, reputable, and currently licensed physician who may assist you in developing a treatment plan that may include a medication regimen.

Emotional

The emotional sub-category of support within my study referred to the single mother having an opportunity to receive counseling and encouragement, or someone to offer sound advice. Emotional support includes seeking both clinical therapy and spiritual counseling. The emotional aspect of support is a key component to establishing and maintaining a strong sense of emotional well-being. As we have discussed in previous chapters, oftentimes, single mothers do not feel that they have people in their corner who understand their reality or may not choose to share the intricacies of their life with others when coming from a mindset that we can do it all without the help of others. Understand that there is a vast difference between venting and having someone vested in your well-being.

Emotional Signs of Disharmony

Have you noticed during the most recent trial, it took a toll on your emotions? Perhaps, you began noticing that worrisome thoughts took over as you constantly thought of the situation, the what ifs, could'ves, should'ves, or if things were or were not in your control, how the situation would change. Have you noticed a veil of sadness just randomly hitting you? Or a dreadful sadness that comes and lasts for an extended period of time, affecting your ability to have a desire to get out of bed most days? Or that time when you felt that you could not breathe or you noticed that you were having frequent panic attacks? These are all indications that you need to develop a plan of self-care. Similar to when physical signs of disharmony occur, it is important to maintain an emotions journey, documenting thoughts, emotions, and associated behavior that may be triggered. It is strongly advised to seek spiritual counseling and clinical therapy with the latter being from a licensed clinician. For those with a preference for a faith-based licensed clinician, know that they do exist. Do your research and interview spiritual counselors and licensed clinicians; as with licensed clinicians, each have a specific style, specialization, and theoretical approach that they gravitate to that you may or may not agree with, so ask these questions prior to engaging in a therapeutic relationship and contract.

Social

Another area of support is the social component. This includes family involvement and support, or the lack thereof, and how this factor impacted their emotional well-being and their parenting.

When looking over the sections of this chapter, understand how the concept of present, intentionality, impact, and support contribute to your emotional well-being. When you decide to move through life, taking advantage of every moment to embrace the present, it truly is one of the most precious you can receive and you can give to others. Being present is the gift of giving of yourself to those most precious, allowing you to serve God's children in the way He has called you to. Being intentional is walking out life on purpose and in God-designed purpose, with intent. And when this begins to take form in your life, you begin to recognize fluff in life. You begin to recognize who and what no longer deserves your time, your energy, or your space. You begin to see life as what it is, precious time that God has given for you to glorify Him and be the vessel He has called you to be. You will be in a place to recognize time-wasters and engage in meaningful connections. Impact is what we have been called to create in whichever realm you find yourself in. In order to be present, intentional, and impactful, it is imperative that one has a positive emotional well-being to show up in the capacity that God has called you to. How is this done? Through various avenues, but one of the most vital components to positive emotional well-being for single mothers is through a strong sense of support, more specifically physical, emotional, and social support.

Practical Application

In this practical application, I challenge you to take inventory of your life, your emotional state, your mindset, and your circle of support. This chapter is to bring various previously discussed concepts to a place of harmony in your life. Research suggests that a level of functional stress is healthy as it creates motivation to strive, to succeed, and to move forward in life. However, a substantial amount of stress can lead to a host of challenges and burnout. If you have experienced this level of stress or feel as though you may be on your way to burnout, we want to stop it in its track right now, in the name of Jesus. In this exercise, make sure that you have prioritized time for yourself to pray, reflect, and journal as God speaks to you. In your journal, I would like you to create a loosely drawn table. On the left side, you are to write each area of your life vertically as though you are listing them, with space in between each area below and space to the right of each topic. These areas include all realms of your life and any specific roles that you play, including motherhood, health, social life, ministry, career, business and entrepreneurship, school for yourself, children's schooling, PTA leader, or any other areas that pertain to your life. Now, move to the top of this list and horizontally write the words *present, intentional,* and *impactful.* In each of the areas and roles that you play in your life, write *how* in detail you are specifically showing up in your life and how you are being present, intentional, and impactful. This exercise may take more than one sitting and that is okay. Do not feel pressured to fill every section to the borders as the point of this exercise is to open your eyes and your heart. Open the door to areas that may need some God-tweaking in your life.

After this task has been completed and you have sought God's wisdom, it is time to move to examining the level of support in your life. On another section of your journal, write down the types of support that you have, write your needs, and if you have support, whether it is sufficient. If it requires modification, how so? What is missing? Who do you have in your life to fill in the support gaps of both your life and your child's life?

Applicable Scriptures

"Be still and know that I am God" (Psalm 46:10).

"Be anxious for nothing, but in everything by prayer and supplication, with thanksgiving, let your requests be made known to God; and the peace of God, which surpasses all understanding, will guard your hearts and minds through Christ Jesus" (Philippians 4:6-7).

"Or do you not know that your body is a temple of the Holy Spirit within you, whom you have from God You are not your own, for you were bought with a price. So glorify God in your body" (1 Corinthians 6:19-20).

"Come to Me, all you who are weary and burdened and I will give you rest. Take My yoke upon you and learn from me, for I am gentle and humble in heart, and you will find rest for your souls. For My yoke is easy and My burden is light" (Matthew 11:28-30).

"The prayer of a righteous man is powerful and effective" (James 5:16).

"So do not fear, for I am with you. Do not be dismayed, for I am your God, I will strengthen you and help you. I will uphold to with My righteous right hand" (Isaiah 41:10).

"God will meet all your needs according to His riches and glory in Christ Jesus" (Philippians 4:9).

"But I urge and entreat you, brethren, by the name of our Lord Jesus Christ, that all of you be in perfect harmony and full agreement in what you say, and that there be no dissensions or factions or divisions among you, but that you be perfectly united in your common understanding and in your opinions and judgments" (1 Corinthians 1:10).

"May grace (God's unmerited favor) and spiritual peace (which means peace with God and harmony, unity, and undisturbedness) be yours from God our Father and from the Lord Jesus Christ" (Ephesians 1:2).

"Be eager and strive earnestly to guard and keep the harmony and oneness of (and produced by) the Spirit in the binding power of peace" (Ephesians 4:3).

"Fill up and complete my joy by living in harmony and being of the same mind and one in purpose, having the same love, being in full accord and of one harmonious mind and intention" (Philippians 2:2).

"And let the peace from Christ rule in your hearts to which as one body you were also called. And be thankful" (Colossians 3:15).

Prayer

Heavenly Father, I'm so grateful for this journey and for this opportunity to draw nearer to You. As You reveal my shortcomings in love and with love, I am choosing to remain faithful, trusting, and vulnerable to You. As I venture on this road to sound emotional well-being, I thank You for opening my eyes to opportunities for growth, to be present, intentional, and impactful in the lives of those You have blessed and entrusted me with. This is the beginning of a new chapter in my life. One in which I am choosing to love me, embrace who I am in You, and pursue peace and harmony. In Jesus' name, amen.

Chapter 10

Conclusion

C O - P A R E N T I N G   W I T H   C H R I S T   I S   M Y   H E A R T ' S
love story of my journey with God as a single mother. I was 20
years-old when I discovered that I was pregnant with my son. I
was in my third year of undergraduate studies. I attended school
by day and worked two jobs in the evenings and on the weekend.
His father and I were not in a long-term relationship and all
communication had ceased. I vividly recall that March night that
I took the pregnancy test. My roommate was not home and a
close high school friend came to visit. My friend stood outside
of the bathroom as I took the pregnancy test. Within minutes,
I slumped to the bathroom floor in tears, and my friend pried
the door open. He quickly sat on the floor next to me, placed his
arms around my upper back as I buried my head into his shoulders. After a few moments, I mumbled a few words and shared
with him how scared I was, what would my parents think, how
was I going to raise my child alone, and that I was not ready. He
held me close and reminded me of how strong I was, that I was
going to be okay, and that I was going to be a good mother. He
whispered in my ear that I was not the type of woman to give
up, and my goals that I set out for three years prior would be
realized as a single mother as well. I would hold onto his words
for years to come.

As the months passed and my belly began to extend, friendships developed and strengthened, relationships were tested,

and life presented a new reality. At five months pregnant, my parents allowed me to move back home. By seven months pregnant, I was attending school full-time, studying on my days off, and working the graveyard shift. At eight months pregnant, my car was rear-ended on the freeway while en route to school. This resulted in me being slightly dilated, no way to get to work, and having to rely on my mother, who kindly drove me to and from my classes. A couple days later, I walked into the department of public social services to apply for public assistance, which I was a recipient of for one year before I requested to terminate the benefits. And one late Saturday night, I gave birth with my parents, my brother, and about ten of my friends in the waiting room. I recall holding this precious being in my arms, terrified of what life held for us. And all in a matter of minutes, a new reality and a norm set in. One week later, my mom dropped me off at school for midterms while she cared for my newborn as she did for many years after. Juggling the many tasks of caring for my son, working, and attending school were challenging. Yet, it developed character. I knew the Lord at that time, but I did not have a relationship with Him until six years later. I would attend church occasionally, had my son in a private school, and had our own place. Yet, I still chose to live life my way. I had settled down compared to my years before I gave birth to my son. However, I had not given my life to Christ until that faithful night of July 27, 2008, when our lives changed forever.

This is when I knew life had to change. I could not explain it and my boyfriend at the time was unsupportive. Yet, something inside of me knew that it was time to open up to God, to the One who I met years before while attending Catholic elementary school. It was the subtle knocking on the door of my heart. The conviction that I felt when I engaged in an ungodly relationship. It was the dream that I had of a man who represented the devil, holding me up, with a ring of fire around us.

In this dream, I began pleading the blood of Jesus and mercy. It was this dream that opened my eyes and opened my heart to Jesus. His grace is sufficient. When I made the decision to open my heart, my life, my home, my family to God, life changed for my son and I. This did not occur overnight, but took years of molding, shaping, and stretching. It involved surrender, vulnerability, humility, and meekness from me. This was the most difficult part of the stretching process. But, my dear sister, this transformation is needed to be able to walk into the life that God has designed, destined, and called you to walk into. This book shares my journey of the good, the difficult, and the growing moments of my life as a woman, mother, and believer.

I say to you reading this book as a single mother, from my heart to yours, from my spirit to yours: being a mother is not easy, being a mother of faith is probably the most difficult challenge that you will face, but it is not impossible, my dear sister. As women, and more specifically, as mothers, we are always giving of ourselves that we seldom leave anything left for us. It is imperative that you feed your spirit, nourish your soul, take care of your body, and stimulate your mind. May it be a few minutes daily or thirty minutes three days weekly, please carve out time for just you and God. Allow Him to use this time to minister to your spirit. He has things to show you, to whisper to you, to teach you, humble you, and most importantly, to grow you. It is okay to be vulnerable to your Maker and allow your tears to wash you clean and free you from any bondage that you may feel, sweet one.

With this said, *Co-parenting with Christ* is meant to walk with you and provide tools on how to achieve harmony in your life in nine steps as a single mother of faith. It is vital that you develop the character of God through identifying who you are in Him, learning what you have been created for and who you have been called to serve, and how to persevere through the challenges of life. These steps provide a foundation. If you are unable to achieve or identify these tools through prayer, journaling, self-reflection, fasting, and worship, it will be difficult to achieve harmony in all areas of your life as a woman of faith. Foundation in your identity in Christ on an individual level paves the way for foundation in your home and family life to take root. It is vital that you sow the seed of faith into your family, sister. This opens the door for the steps of structure in your home, open communication with your children, and paradigm shift in your view of your role as a mother and as a romantic helpmate. These steps contribute to creating harmony in your life. Foundation on an individual level and foundation on a familial level leads to your ability to discern clarity. Clarity comes through listening and hearing the voice of God. A secure and confident woman of God who knows who she is in Christ, what she carries within her, her understanding of the power and influence she bears, and the legacy she leaves behind is a godly force to be reckoned with. Do not strive for perfection as we are perfectly imperfect in Him, and He loves us. He loves you, sweet one. More than you may ever know. I hope you enjoyed this journey that we embarked on together, and when life feels a tad uncomfortable, you may review sections of this book or re-read to get stirred up again. So until next time, sister, take care of yourself, be kind to yourself, and love yourself and your family to life. And even more importantly, allow God to love you.

Prayer

If you do not know the Lord, if you do not have a relationship with God, if you are not a born-again believer, or if you lost your way and need to come back, then read the following prayer:

Father, I come humbly before the Throne of Grace. I thank you for the season you have me in at this moment, but I know that I have not fully surrendered my heart and my life to You. I hear You knocking on the door of my heart, and I will not allow fear, discomfort, inconvenience, or distractions to keep me from having a relationship with You. I am not praying to join a religion, but to establish a relationship with You. I no longer wish to be a little bit in and a little out. I desire to have an authentic relationship with You. I am a sinner. I have sinned, and I ask You to forgive me for my sins. I repent. I am choosing to give my life wholeheartedly to You, Jesus. I relinquish the reins over my life, and I fully surrender to You. I give You Lordship over my life and over my heart. Jesus, I ask You to be my Lord and Savior. Thank You, Father, for sending Your Son, Jesus, to die for our sins. Thank You for loving me as only You can. In Jesus' name, I pray. Amen.

About The Author

DR. CHANEL SERANO IS A FAITH-BASED author, speaker, entrepreneur, influencer, blogger, and ministry leader based in Southern California. She is a solo parent and shares a home with her young adult son, Isaiah, and feisty German Shepherd. Dr. Serano has a master of arts, a doctor of education degree in counseling psychology, and is currently pursuing licensure. She has been in social services and the helping profession for over two decades and currently serves in a leadership capacity in the governmental sector. She also serves as a college instructor, teaching social sciences. And she leads a faith-based single mothers ministry, both within the church walls and within the community.

Her blog site, www.doinglifewithchristblog.wordpress.com, helps women and single moms of faith strengthen their identity in Christ, learn effective strategies on how to lead a solo parent household, how to identify and walk in God-designed purpose, and serve in the leadership capacity in the home, boardroom, community, and ministry. Furthermore, Dr. Serano is the founder of Esther's Daughters, an LLC geared towards providing faith-based parenting curriculum for single moms, curriculum for faith-based organizations interested in developing the tools to implement a faith-based single moms parenting program, books and other literary work geared toward single moms, and online courses and webinars to equip single moms in various seasons of their single mom journey.

Dr. Serano enjoys spending quality time with her son and loved ones, conducting research, writing, attending and hosting workshops, and jogging! To learn more about solo parenting curricula, workshops, courses, and speaking engagements, contact Dr. Serano at the aforementioned blog. You may also connect with her on all social media platforms under *Doing Life with Christ: Living with Intention* and *Esther's Daughters.* For speaking engagement requests, you may contact Dr. Serano and her team at Dr.chanelserano@gmail.com.

References

Baumrind, Diana. 1967. "Child Care Practices Anteceding Three Patterns of Preschool Behavior." *Genetic Psychology Monographs,* 75, no. 1: 43–88.

Bea, Scott. 2016. "Wanna Give? This Is Your Brain on a 'Helper's High'." Accessed 2019. https://health.cleveland-clinic.org/why-giving-is-good-for-your-health/.

Black, Bernadette and Fred J. Hecklinger. 2006. *Training for Life: A Practical Guide to Career and Life Planning.* 9th ed. Dubuque: Kendall/Hunt Publishing Group.

Bristow, Jennie, Charlotte Faircloth, Ellie Lee, and Jan Macvarish. 2014. *Parenting Culture Studies.* Basingstoke: Palgrave Macmillan.

Centers for Disease Control and Prevention. 2019. *Preventing Adverse Childhood Experiences (ACEs): Leveraging the Best Available Evidence.* Atlanta, GA: National Center for Injury Prevention and Control, Centers for Disease Control and Prevention.

Deaton, Angus and Daniel Kahneman. 2010. High Income Improves Evaluation of Life not Emotional Well-being. *Proceedings of the National Academy of Sciences of the United States of America,* 107, no. 38: 16489-16493.

Doran, George T. "There's a S.M.A.R.T. Way to Write Management's Goals and Objectives." *Management Review,* 70, no. 11: 35-36.

Erikson, Erik. 1959. *Identity and the Life Cycle.* New York: W.W. Norton & Company.

Eyberg, Sheila, Jane Querido, and Tamara Warner. 2002. "Parenting Styles and Child Behavior in African American Families of Preschool Children." *Journal of Clinical Child & Adolescent Psychology*, 31, no. 2: 272-7.

Gaille, Brandon. 2017. "23 Interesting Permissive Parenting Statistics." Accessed 2020. https://brandongaille. com/21-interesting-permissive-parenting-statistics/#:~:- text=%20%20%201%20Children%20who%20experi- ence%20a,parent%E2%80%99s%20queues%20in%20 regards%20to%20problematic...%20More

Leifer, Gloria and Eve Fleck. 2013. *Growth and Development: Across the Lifespan*. 2nd ed. St. Louis: Elsevier Inc.

Merriam-Webster.com Dictionary, s.v. "structure," accessed November 25, 2020, https://www.merriam-webster.com/ dictionary/structure

Schnarr, Ashley, Tracey Ferrell, Sarah Mae, and Darlene Schacht. 2013. *Single Girl*. 2nd ed. St. Louis: Ashley Schnarr.

Takieddine, Nora Sabahat. "Self-Differentiation and Why It Matters in Families and Relationships" *Good*

Therapy. August 31, 2017. https://www.goodtherapy.org/blog/ self-differentiation-why-it-matters-in-families-relation- ships-0831174.

CPSIA information can be obtained
at www.ICGtesting.com
Printed in the USA
LVHW050035160321
681579LV00018B/170